WITHDRAWN

Manage Your
REMODEL

AND SAVE MONEY!

D1361409

CRE🏠TIVE
HOMEOWNER®

MANAGE YOUR
REMODEL

AND *SAVE MONEY!*

VICTORIA LIKES

CREATIVE HOMEOWNER®, Upper Saddle River, New Jersey

MANAGE YOUR REMODEL

AUTHOR	Victoria Likes
MANAGING EDITOR	Fran Donegan
EDITOR	Lisa Kahn
PROOFREADING	Sara M. Markowitz
PHOTO COORDINATOR	Mary Dolan
DIGITAL IMAGING SPECIALIST	Frank Dyer
INDEXER	Schroeder Indexing Services
DESIGN AND LAYOUT	David Geer
COVER PHOTOGRAPHY	Eli Brownell; Victoria Likes (inset)
INTERIOR PHOTOGRAPHY	Eli Brownell (finished shots); Victoria Likes (construction shots)
ILLUSTRATIONS	Clarke Barre (pp.160–161)

CREATIVE HOMEOWNER

VICE PRESIDENT AND PUBLISHER	Timothy O. Bakke
MANAGING EDITOR	Fran J. Donegan
ART DIRECTOR	David Geer
PRODUCTION COORDINATOR	Sara M. Markowitz

Current Printing (last digit)
10 9 8 7 6 5 4 3 2 1

Manufactured in the United States of America

Manage Your Remodel, First Edition
Library of Congress Control Number: 2008941325
ISBN-10: 1-58011-434-2
ISBN-13: 978-1-58011-434-9

CREATIVE HOMEOWNER®
A Division of Federal Marketing Corp.
24 Park Way
Upper Saddle River, NJ 07458
www.creativehomeowner.com

ACKNOWLEDGMENTS

This book is dedicated to my husband, Bart—without whose intelligence, guidance, encouragement, and backbreaking work, neither our own remodel, nor the writing of this book could have happened. To you, and everyone else out there ready to take the plunge, here's to that first glass of wine in an unfinished kitchen.

Also to my father, who at age 78 continues to embrace new challenges and inspires me to do more, be more, and learn more, no matter what the subject.

Thanks also to my sister Tamra Lynn Cooper, who successfully test-drove many of the management ideas and techniques listed here on her home remodel. Thanks also to Eli Brownell, who provided the inspiring and beautiful "after" photographs.

I am also grateful for all the patience, skill, and expertise of those I had the honor of working with on both the remodel and in the publication of this book. They endured countless hours of questioning, kept me out of harm's way, opened my eyes to the world of construction, and showed a spirit of partnership in both action and word. They're the true experts and the voice of experience, and you can trust that they, or others like them, would serve you well. Heartfelt thanks to each of you:

Pete Sandall, Sandall Norrie Architects; Gregory Coons, Swenson Say Faget Engineering; Earl Williams, Williams Construction; Carl Hayes, CNC Plumbing; Steve Breen, APlus Remoal Systems; Craig Chaussee, Roof Truss Supply, Inc; Lorna Redwood, Woodinville Cabinet & Millwork Inc; Paul Brown, Quality Tile & Marble; Valeriy Korol, Val's Construction; Carlos Milan, Milan Marble & Granite; Larry Howard, Legacy Roofing; Rodd Walker, Blue Flame Heating & Air Conditioning; Rick Jones, Galeed Concrete Relationships LLC; Mike Rodgers, Pella Northwest; Paul Danis, Emerald State Drywall; Aaron Vanek, Luna Park Construction; Eduardo Contreras, EJ Painting Contracting; Skip King, Manager, Construction Inspections, City of Seattle Department of Planning and Development; Debora Prinz, King County, Washington, Residential Assessor's Office.

CONTENTS

INTRODUCTION

Your home is a true reflection of who you are. Your preferences for its size, design, and adornment reveal your deepest values. It's a place where life unfolds, where comfort is found, and where those you love gather, grow, and share.

IT'S LIKELY THAT THE PLACE YOU CALL HOME is also the most valuable asset you own. So it's not surprising that altering it with an upgrade, addition, or a complete renovation takes courage as well as cash.

The decision to remodel can feel even riskier if you choose to manage your project yourself. Yet this is not really as radical as it sounds. After all, people have been building their homes from the ground up, by hand, using available local materials since the dawn of civilization.

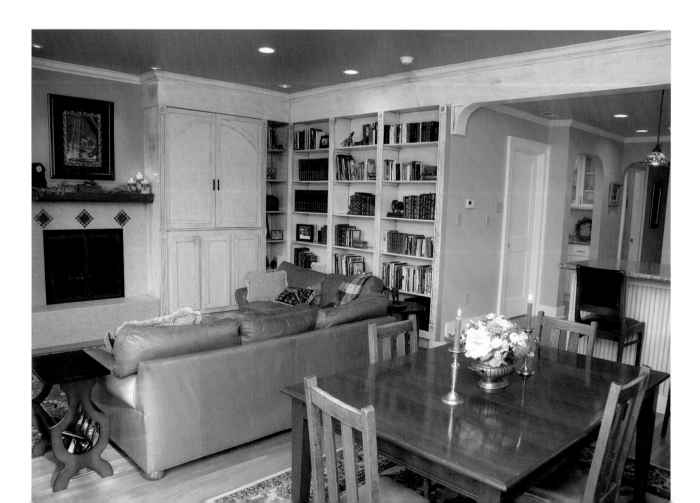

According to the National Association of Home Builders, we spent $226.4 billion on home improvement in 2007, and much of that money came from the pockets of do-it-yourselfers. In today's economy, homeowners have more bargaining power than we've had in years. If you are willing to go out into your neighborhood and look around, you'll find a wide range of skilled craftsmen. With their help, you will be able to create a home that truly reflects your lifestyle and taste—and save money in the process.

This book will tell you exactly what you need to know to succeed as the HGC (Homeowner General Contractor) of your own home-remodeling project. Not because you can't afford to hire a professional general contractor, but because you understand that every dollar you save by doing it yourself is an extra dollar you can invest in your dream home.

With a little understanding and the techniques I learned from my own experience as an

HOW TO USE THIS BOOK

MANAGE YOUR REMODEL AND SAVE is really two books. It provides you with the information you need to take the reins and become the general contractor on your own remodeling project. But it also tells the story of the remodeling project that Victoria Likes undertook on her Seattle home. As you read the text, you will be learning what Victoria learned through her on-the-job training. Look for the large type to see the important lessons she learned. Of course, every major project has its challenges, and Victoria's was no exception. She reveals some of those problems and how she handled them in the "Learning Curve" sidebars throughout the book. All of the photos are of Victoria's house, taken either during construction or when finally finished. Sometimes we grouped them together to show how persistence, focus, and hard work pay off in the end. —*The Editors*

HGC, I will show you how to manage your own project and save 20 to 30 percent on your remodeling costs. I'll also explain how to get many extras, such as higher-quality materials, unique features, and just plain square footage that you would not have access to if you hired a professional to oversee your project.

Managing a remodel is a remarkable adventure. In the big scheme of things, there's a beginning, middle, and end to your work. And you will eventually get to a place where you can step back and say, "It's absolutely perfect." But in the thick of it, there's much to do, all of the time. And you just have to know that going in.

Finally, I wanted to show off, just a little, the home we remodeled and restored. I had little experience when I started the project, and I made a few mistakes. Still, it turned out beautifully, and it will remain an enduring triumph in our life. I think everyone is entitled to that kind of fun.

CHAPTER 1

WHAT ARE YOU GETTING INTO?

- LEARN WHAT IT TAKES TO MANAGE YOUR REMODELING PROJECT

- GET A BRIEF GLIMPSE OF THE DIFFERENT TASKS THAT WILL BE REQUIRED OF YOU

- GUARANTEE YOUR SUCCESS BY CHOOSING CONSTRUCTION PROFESSIONALS WITH THE RIGHT CREDENTIALS

Taking the Leap

*A few years ago, before home improvement shows became such a huge trend,
I hadn't the slightest idea of what lay hidden behind the walls of where I lived. It wasn't
until life threw a dilapidated 1925 Colonial Revival bungalow into my lap that I
first saw the bones and heart of a house.*

Of all the things I've learned in managing my own remodel, I've been most impressed by how many hands shape the place we call home. So many lives cross paths in the exposed landscape of a house torn apart; leaving behind layer upon layer of carefully measured and applied materials.

Remodeling a house is similar in many ways to a team working on a complicated puzzle. You ponder stairwells with the framer, rooflines with the architect, tile layout with the tile setter, and cabinetry with the finish carpenter. Each professional adds the right piece in the right place until the puzzle is complete and you have a home.

Don't waste your time by RE-REMODELING.
Do it right the first time.

CREATING YOUR DESIGN SCHEME

NO ONE IS BETTER QUALIFIED than you to know how you want to live. But as you begin to imagine your dream home, remember that you'll need to convey your ideas to the people who are going to help make it happen. This brings me to the first rule of managing your remodel: commit your plan to paper.

Typically, a building plan is produced by an architect who translates your ideas into working drawings and then helps you file them with your local building department for review and approval. There are also times when you may require the help of other professionals, such as a surveyor or engineer, before you end up with a final design.

If your project is tiny, your plan can be as simple as a handmade drawing. But if the work involves anything that may impact your home's structural integrity, assume that you will need professional help.

MASTER BEDROOM: We always dreamed of a small deck off the master bedroom.

The General Contractor's Job. No doubt you've heard that the role of a general contractor is to supervise and direct the work of others. As the general contractor you will not be sawing, swinging a hammer, or pouring concrete—unless you really want to. You will be in charge of those trades, but your job will be much bigger than just managing a construction crew. There are a host of other responsibilities, many of which occur even before you break ground.

My Experience. Choosing to manage my own project has transformed me from a fairly helpless homeowner into someone capable of finding a real solution. No more hiding nailholes with pictures, repainting water stains on the ceiling, or rearranging furniture to mask a buckled floor. Now I know that everything in a house is fixable with a steady hand, patience, and some talent—all of which may be bought at a decent price. The trick is how you, as the person in charge, can successfully manage the work. And that's what this book is all about.

If you decide to manage your remodel yourself, you'll likely get more value built into your home. That's because the money you save by not hiring a professional general contractor can be used for upgrades or savings that you can pocket yourself. Don't underestimate the complexity of the work before you, however. Even a "minor" project can contain many steps. You'll also be dealing with tradespeople who may sometimes test your patience and interpersonal skills. Knowing what's expected of you, and what you can expect from others, will make the difference between stumbling through—or achieving success.

Managing Costs

If you ask an experienced subcontractor to provide you with a bid on a project, he'll naturally include materials, along with the acquisition, transport, and labor costs he expects to incur. It's standard business practice to mark up the entire bid to make a profit.

What this means is that if you buy the materials yourself and hire the contractor only for the labor, you will save money. Why? Because you'll comparison shop to get better-quality materials at a lower price. You'll also compare the bids for labor from a number of subcontractors. In this way you'll quickly come to understand what labor and materials actually cost. And knowing what work

needs to done, by which professional, using what kinds of materials is what your job is all about.

A Range of Responsibilities. For a simple bathroom remodel, you may need demolition workers to remove the old surfaces and fixtures, a plumber, a drywall professional, a painter, and possibly a tile setter to install the new tile. You will also purchase all of the materials, including the cabinetry, a tub, a sink, shower, faucets, paint, tile, and towel racks. When you manage your own remodel, you're responsible for selecting and purchasing the materials, and then arranging to have them delivered—or hauling them home yourself.

In addition to saving money, there is another advantage to purchasing all of the materials and products for your project: you get to shake up the rules about what should be used or how to put things together. Amazing new products from around the world are just a click away on your computer. As your own boss, you have the opportunity to create and innovate as much as you like.

It helps not to hate shopping because you'll probably be buying materials until the final day of your project.

Learning Curve

When a Bargain Is No Bargain

There was one instance during my project when I felt uneasy about a potential work arrangement. This happened early in the game in the form of a tile worker and his helper.

Apparently they had seen the construction from the street and had come in to meet me in order to land the job. They claimed to be experts in their field, although neither owned an actual business. Deciding to take a chance, I invited them to walk through the house, figuring that I'd check their credentials later.

As we went from room to room, I noticed they didn't ask any questions or jot down notes, and they asserted a little too confidently that they could do everything I wanted—no problem.

By the time we were upstairs, I finally asked the lead worker how he was going to deliver a bid if he hadn't written anything down. Without blinking an eye, he offered to do the job for a price that was $10,000 less than all of my other bids. What's more, he could start the next day.

Wow! That certainly sounded like a good deal, I thought. Still, I wondered, why so cheap? I soon got my answer.

"So, how would you approach this?" I asked, as I showed the boss a complicated plan for a shower wall.

"Oh, I won't be doing the work myself. Todd here will," he replied as he turned to his helper, who grinned and nodded. "Yeah, I did a shower on another job and it was no problem."

"Just one?" I asked.

"Well, I've done a lot of tile work in my career. I've been doing it since ... last summer or so," he said as he glanced nervously at his partner. At that point, I escorted them to the door.

I now know that these two had all the signs of "When a Bargain Is No Bargain." And if you're ever tempted by an offer that seems too good to be true, here are some things that should set off your alarm bells:

- Anyone quoting an exceptionally low price without putting it in writing.

- An overconfident, "can do" attitude that doesn't correspond with the complexity of the project.

- Immediate availability. Reputable contractors typically aren't that quickly obtainable.

- When the individual handling the money isn't the one doing the work. That spells all kinds of trouble—including the possibility that he won't pay the actual tradesman, who could then walk off the job and leave you in the lurch!

Here's a small sample of the work performed by the tile subcontractor who did get the job.

Avoid Impulsive Decisions

One trait that is essential to a good general contractor is the ability to see the big picture. There are many moving parts to construction projects. Snap judgments, impulsive purchases, and wasting time are just a few of the pitfalls for the first-timer.

General contracting requires thinking about your goals, evaluating your options, and being smart about what constitutes a "bargain." Be warned: almost everyone will want you to believe that they have a bargain— just for you. It's your job to separate the few real bargains from the many offers that aren't.

In general, it's not a bargain when:

- It sounds too good to be true.

- You end up doing twice or three times the work for a minimal payoff.

- Cost is the only factor guiding a purchasing or hiring decision.

SECURING THE PERMITS

IN ORDER TO SECURE a master building permit, you or your architect must submit your plans to the local building department. If the project requires a plumber, electrician, or heating-and-air-conditioning contractor, you'll also need a special permit for each of these. Regardless of whether you or your subcontractor secures these permits, it's your responsibility to make sure that all of the necessary permits and inspections are in order so that your work meets (or exceeds) local building codes.

Finding the Money

As the general contractor, it's your job to find the financing for your project. Whether it's through savings, a loan, or cashing out another asset, you'll need enough money to pay for all aspects of your remodel project, plus a cushion for the unexpected. Once you've lined up your financing, you're responsible for distributing all of the funds as needed to workers and vendors until the job is completed.

A word of warning: don't knock down any walls until you have arranged for the money you'll need to complete your project. Banks won't lend on a demolished home, no matter how glorious your plans for completion may be. Most home loan documents contain language that prohibits you from destroying your home without au-

To obtain the home you want, be sure that all of the financing is in place before you start the project.

thorization from the lender. Few lenders snoop around for unauthorized home demolitions, of course. But if you run out of money mid-remodel, you may have some problems. The bank will not be pleased that you've created an uninhabitable home out of a once-intact asset, which, technically, belongs to them until you pay off your mortgage.

Everyone you hire must have these three characteristics:

They must be accountable.
They must be professional.
They must be experienced.

Hiring, Scheduling, and Managing

You'll need workers to handle nearly every aspect of your job, from demolition and debris removal to finish carpentry and painting. If you forget to hire someone, trust me—the others will definitely let you know when something isn't their job. Fortunately, they'll also be happy to tell you whose job it is. At the most basic level, you will be looking for workers who are **accountable, professional,** and **experienced.**

An *accountable* **subcontractor** owns his own business, and cares about his reputation. He takes ownership of his work and won't hesitate to guarantee you a satisfactory outcome. He takes pride in his skills and is capable of successfully completing his portion of the job and then handing it off to the next contractor in line. As a result, he will work with you to make sure that you are happy and will provide you with options or concessions if you're not.

SITE SERVICES & SAFETY

UNLESS YOU ARE WILLING to share your bathroom with the work crew, it is your responsibility as the general contractor to provide them with alternative toilet facilities. You'll also need to arrange for electricity for their tools, a place to store equipment and supplies, a dumpster, and possibly, a temporary fence around your property. This last one will not only keep curious neighbors out but also eliminate topsoil run off. It's also the general contractor's job to provide a first-aid kit and to make sure that workers adhere to standard safety practices, such as wearing safety goggles or using proper construction protocol. In some cases, you may want to purchase additional homeowner's insurance to protect yourself in the event of an accident.

Learning Curve

Finding Out the Hard Way

There's much to pay attention to on a construction site. It's often a hazard-filled, cluttered place with uneven ground, overhead obstructions, and nails, staples, and pointed tools everywhere. Little did I know just how dangerous it could be until we embarked on our own project.

One morning, hours before anyone else arrived, I was walking along the footings at the back of the house. I must not have been paying attention because, suddenly, my foot caught under a piece of stray lumber and I took a tumble. Luckily I didn't hit anything sharp, because exposed rebar was everywhere. The only thing injured was my pride, which turned out to be a good thing.

Several weeks later, I heard a horrifying story of a worker on another job who had been impaled on a piece of rebar. Mind you, this was a professional—someone who had spent most of his adult life on construction sites. Fortunately, he had surgery and eventually returned to work.

So please, make sure that exposed dangers are clearly marked and proper protections put in place. For rebar, that means adding safety caps. Pay attention, and watch your step—especially when you're alone. Help could be a long time coming.

A *professional* **subcontractor** doesn't just say he knows how to do the work; he actually does it for a living. When you hire a professional, you hire both his skills and his knowledge of the industry. This means that you don't have to be a construction or building code expert—you just have to manage and oversee someone who is.

An *experienced* **subcontractor** has been doing his job long enough to know most of the landmines and pitfalls. That experience will help you avoid mistakes, make improvements, and save time and money through all kinds of efficiencies—and it won't cost you an extra penny.

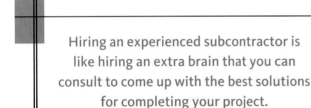

Hiring an experienced subcontractor is like hiring an extra brain that you can consult to come up with the best solutions for completing your project.

The construction industry is filled with experienced people, so why in the world would you hire someone who doesn't know how to do his job? Experience adds value, and the smart homeowner chooses that experience over the less-expensive novice every time.

Making Decisions. Every day, you'll be asked questions about how you want to proceed with the work. Issues big and small will arise—crooked walls, uneven foundations, and off-kilter fixtures—and you'll be directing your crew to compensate, based on their opinions, your architect's input, and your own best judgment. This is a role that, depending upon your personality, either will be quite rewarding or will drive you nuts. If it turns out to be the latter, remember, the work won't last forever, and with a little patience, you can manage through.

Juggling and Multitasking

Managing a remodel is like making sausage. The process isn't pretty, but everybody loves the outcome.

Construction is not a desk job. You need to be seen and heard while you manage a wide range of different issues and concerns. To save valuable time, plan on doing a good portion of that work on the hoof and in the field. Sometimes that means you just have to check in at several points during the day to make sure your workers have shown up, have started on the day's work, and are still progressing well at noon. At other times, you might have to stay longer, perhaps to call together your larger team of professionals to address a problem or issue. In addition, the time it takes to design, plan, obtain permits, select and purchase materials, hire and manage workers, and oversee and orchestrate the project is considerable. Your management responsibilities are ongoing; time-comsuming; and all-inclusive.

Knowledge Is Power. Good general contractors, by nature, want to know everything they can about a remodeling project upfront. The type of work involved, the finishes, the cabinetry, and other materials needed to complete the job will dictate the project's cost and determine the profit margin. Good general contractors also strive to have all of their i's dotted and t's crossed before construction starts so that the bids they get from their suppliers and subcontractors will result in an accurate project cost. Once work is underway, the general contractor's goal is to follow the established plan, because changes in construction cost money and have a ripple effect on the rest of the project. Managing a remodel is as much about managing the planning and design as it is about overseeing on-site construction.

The Importance of Scheduling. You'll need to pay close attention to subcontractor ordering and delivery timelines in order to keep your project on schedule. If you've ever heard about a construction project that went on for months—or even years—beyond the planned

Your time commitment is in direct proportion to the size of the project. You must be ready to drop everything and run to your job site at a moment's notice to make a critical decision, provide materials, or powwow with your team to keep things on track.

completion date, it most likely had something to do with poor scheduling. Not only will you set the dates for completion of work—and monitor your workers to ensure that they meet those dates—but you'll also schedule the handoff between different subcontractors. Sequencing and orchestrating the work between the various trades and ensuring that each one delivers a completed product to the next is a key ingredient of a successful project.

But regardless of whether you manage the entire project yourself, hire someone to do it for you, or even partner with a construction business veteran to serve as your advisor while you manage the project, this book will explain what's involved, and how you, or your chosen representative, will accomplish the tasks of transforming the house you have today into the home you've always wanted to own.

The general contractor's responsibilities may seem overwhelming, but with patience, perseverance, and a little luck, your project will go from the mayhem of a construction site to your dream home.

CHAPTER 2

DEFINING YOUR DREAM

IN THIS CHAPTER

- DETERMINE WHETHER REMODELING IS THE RIGHT CHOICE FOR YOU

- LEARN MORE ABOUT THE DUTIES OF A GENERAL CONTRACTOR

- CREATE YOUR REMODELING WISH LIST

Decision Time

This chapter will help you get from "I think I'd like to remodel my home," to "I'm ready to go!" But there are a few decisions to make first, and the most important is deciding whether remodeling is the right choice for you. Start by listing your ideas. You can't get in over your head simply by putting ideas down on paper. The only thing you have to lose is your uncertainty.

Is My Home Worth Remodeling?

If you've practiced the real estate mantra, "Location, Location, Location," maybe you've purchased a home that's in a desirable neighborhood, even though the house is outdated or lacks the space you require. If you're situated on the right lot or your home has some elements you'd like to retain, remodeling can be the right course of action. But not every home is a good candidate for a remodel. Sometimes moving or tearing the house down and rebuilding from scratch is the appropriate solution.

Very few people deliberately purchase a home they plan to knock down. However, investing in a radical renovation of a house that's not worth saving in the first place isn't smart, either. In this case, you may be better off—financially as well as emotionally—by moving or completely starting over. That's because the cost of re-modeling, per square foot, can be considerably higher than the cost of new construction.

So before you make any final decisions, consider all of your options. The last thing you need is a fully remodeled home that you still don't like. An Internet resource worth checking out is **www.remodelormove.com,** which provides a calculator that helps you weigh the pros and cons of remodeling versus moving.

You will also need to commit to the time involved. If you're considering a major renovation, better plan on spending between four and nine months on researching, developing, and getting permits for the project—before you begin construction. This gives you time to study different designs, figure out your likes and dislikes, evaluate architectural and construction issues, and develop complete working drawings. If your project is small—perhaps a single room—expect to spend up to two months on the development process.

BASEMENT: We wanted to convert part of the basement into a stand-alone apartment with its own entrance.

SHOULD YOU REMODEL YOUR HOME **(do it)**, re-build from scratch **(do-it-over)**, or simply pack up and move **(move it)**? The smart homeowner carefully considers all the possibilities before making such an important decision. Answering these questions can help you determine the course of action that's right for you.

■ Does your house have historical significance or original features that you'd like to retain? **(Do it.)**

■ Does your house have a platform—such as a solid foundation and a main floor—that you can build upon? **(Do it.)**

■ Would moving into another home in your neighborhood that better suits your needs be more affordable than remodeling your existing home? **(Move it.)**

■ Do you love your neighborhood/garden/driveway or view so much that you absolutely must stay put, no matter what? **(Do it** or **do-it-over.)**

■ Would you need to spend a lot on the exterior of your home to give it charm and curb appeal? External renovations can be expensive and provide you with little or no lifestyle improvement within the house. **(Move it** or **do-it-over.)**

■ Does your remodel plan require completely taking the house apart? **(Move it, do-it-over,** or—if you're really prepared to bite the bullet—**do it** in order to save the one part of the house that you really love.)

What Exactly Will You Change?

Ask yourself if any of the following apply to you:

1. Are there too few bathrooms to comfortably accommodate everyone in the household?

2. Do you lack room for all your furniture and other possessions? Are they spilling over onto the porch or garage or into the local storage facility?

3. Do you have to leave the house to re-enter the basement in order to reach the laundry area?

4. Is your kitchen outdated, cramped, or dingy?

Consider What You Will Use. After you've listed the obvious problems, as well as minor concerns such as paint color on walls or a sloping kitchen floor, it's time to compare the way you live now with the way you'd truly like to live. For example, if you've always dreamed of having a bowling alley in your home, now is the time to give the idea some serious consideration. Perhaps you're a professional bowler, and your entire family plays on a regular basis. In this case, a home bowling alley might be a practical, life-enhancing addition.

If you think this is an extreme example, compare it to the formal dining room: while it is incorporated into many homes, this room may get only one or two special-occasion uses per year. Would a dining room be a wise investment for your home, or would the space be more useful as, say, a home office? The reality is that most of us can only afford to include those modifications that will be the most useful to our family most of the time.

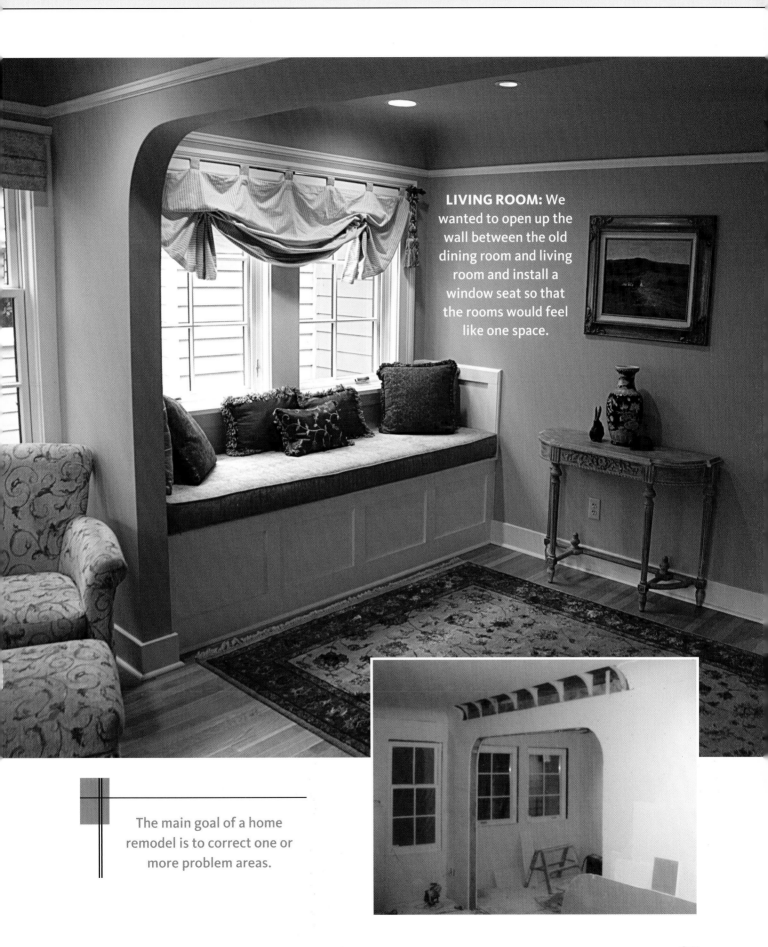

LIVING ROOM: We wanted to open up the wall between the old dining room and living room and install a window seat so that the rooms would feel like one space.

The main goal of a home remodel is to correct one or more problem areas.

Learning Curve

Why We Remodeled

When my young son and I first moved back to Seattle, after a Jerry Springer-style divorce that took way too long, my goal was to land in one of the area's small, attractive 1920s bungalows. I envisioned a wide front window, a generous porch, and just enough space to feel safe and secure on my lone remaining sofa.

One such house—complete with a silly turret that melted my heart with its cockeyed confidence—stood out from the rest. However, it did have a few warts. Almost everything needed to be replaced; the layout was unworkable; and space was tight. (I convinced myself that it was "cozy.")

Still, the house's benefits far outweighed its drawbacks. The setting was perfect—just 10 minutes from downtown Seattle in a nice neighborhood with sidewalks for my 8-year-old son to ride his bicycle. And so we had a home.

Fast-forward this scene four years; add a new husband, two dogs, and a pair of lounging teenagers (mine

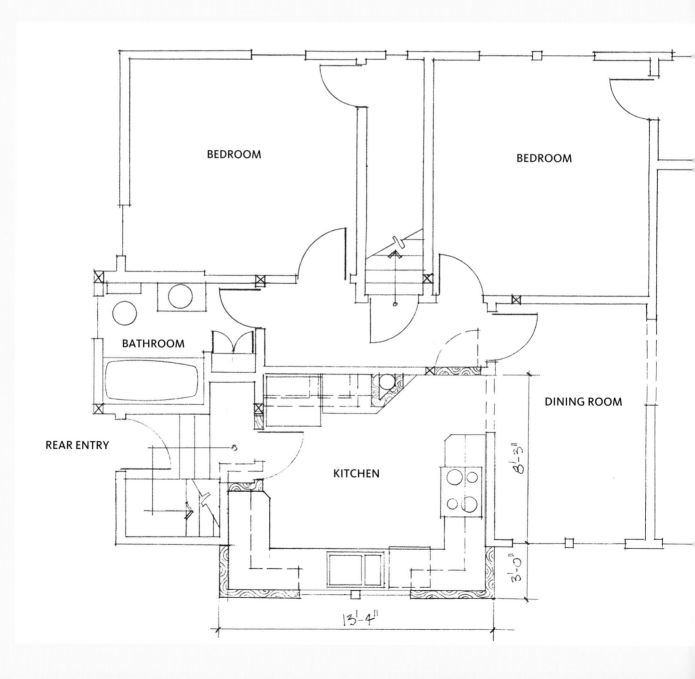

plus a stepson). Not only was my newly enlarged family pinched for space, but the cramped floor plan created some truly unpleasant moments—especially when we had guests. For instance, you could sit on the sofa in the living room and look down the length of the house. The kitchen was on one side, bedrooms on the other; and at the end of the hall was an unobstructed view of the toilet. Lord help anyone who didn't lock the door!

The house as it stood couldn't survive our new family arrangement. To gain the living space we desperately needed, we had to rearrange almost every room—and add a few more, besides.

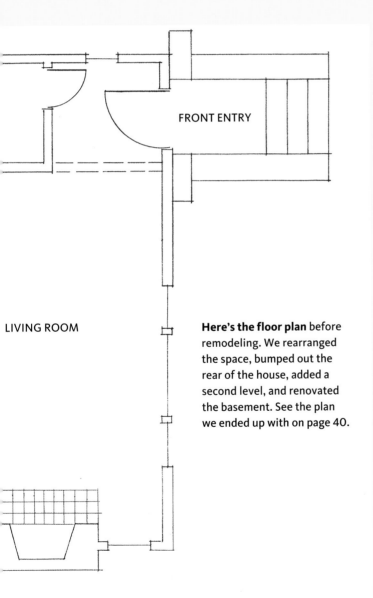

FRONT ENTRY

LIVING ROOM

Here's the floor plan before remodeling. We rearranged the space, bumped out the rear of the house, added a second level, and renovated the basement. See the plan we ended up with on page 40.

Building-In Resale Value

Talk to any homeowner in the middle of a remodel, and they're likely to tell you that they plan to stay put forever. This belief has often helped to justify some pretty unusual or costly improvements.

The truth is that the average homeowner moves every five to seven years, or about 11 times in his or her lifetime. In other words, no matter what you think your future plans might be, you must consider how your renovation will affect the resale value of your home. If you should ever put your home on the market, one of its key selling points will be its exterior facade, or "curb appeal."

Adding Curb Appeal. If you're familiar with home improvement shows, you know that houses with curb appeal attract buyers. However, what's important is that the design and scope of the enhancements don't exceed the value of other homes in the neighborhood. Your goal is to create a more enjoyable and useful space for yourself while leveraging your home's marketability for the future.

Should you decide to sell later, a potential buyer can gather information on your home through the local tax assessment office. In addition to tax data, this office also rates the condition of your home relative to its age and lists the value of any improvements you've made.

Because it's in everyone's best interest to keep your home in the best condition possible, some states encourage upgrades by offering a temporary tax exemption on the portion of your home that is being remodeled. It pays to check with your local assessor's office to see whether you are eligible for such an exemption.

Determining Your Style

A renovation can go very wrong when it isn't consistent with the home's original style or when two disparate styles are merged together. In other words, if you own a charming bungalow-style home, you'll get the best results if your remodel respects your home's original spirit and character.

What style of remodel would best suit both you and your house? Get some inspiration by researching a variety of options.

- Attend open houses and other real estate events.

- Drive through neighborhoods to identify homes you like; make notes about specific details that appeal to you.

- Regularly peruse magazines, books, and the Internet for pictures of rooms and features you like; then assemble a file for later reference.

- Visit regional home shows.

- Check out kitchen, plumbing, flooring, and cabinet showrooms in your area.

Do Your Research. During this phase of your analysis, you'll also begin to grasp what is required to accomplish the work. Let's use the bungalow example again. Perhaps you want to add a new room onto the front of your house, but you haven't considered extending the roofline over the new addition.

Had you not discovered through your research that a wide, overhanging eave is the hallmark of a bungalow-style home, you might have faced big problems later on. Knowing about that roof extension is critical if you want an accurate estimate of your project costs before the work begins. Add it after construction starts, and the cost will at least double.

Over time, you'll become more familiar with the key components of your home's architectural style. Once your project is underway, you'll find that using a picture to explain your ideas to either the architect, a supplier, or a subcontractor is quite helpful.

Make a Wish List. As you figure out your style, make a list of the architectural details you hope to include. It's critical to have this information in advance because the cost of your remodel will be directly affected by this wish list. Share your desire for custom tile or vaulted ceilings with the subcontractors you invite to bid on the project.

ACTING LIKE SHERLOCK HOLMES

A LARGE-SCALE REMODEL requires an enormous amount of decision making and much to purchase. The keys to figuring out the best solutions and finding the best deals lie in your tenacity and thoroughness.

Take on the task of planning your home remodel the same way Sherlock Holmes takes on a murder investigation—engage in some good, old-fashioned sleuthing.

The process of searching for facts and information keeps you carefully cautious. It can also lead to more interesting options and choices than you previously imagined. For example, you may find that what you're looking for is available at more than one place, can be purchased at a lower price, or could possibly be custom-made for a reasonable price.

It probably comes as no surprise that the Internet is the number-one resource for finding what you need to buy for your project. But you'll also need to follow up your online research with phone calls, emails, and visits to suppliers, stores, and showrooms.

Otherwise, you're likely to miss critical construction requirements, such as the proper framing to support tile or create a coved ceiling. Your construction and materials bids will be way off base, and you'll be in a constant state of "change orders."

How do you know whether your newly hatched ideas will work with your existing home? Seek out and talk to every home-design and building professional that you encounter. When you've heard something repeated enough times, you might be willing to step back from your original plan and modify it to suit the industry standard. It's a good bet you'll end up with a better looking, better designed home.

Try to get a feel not only for the elements contained in each room but also for how your rooms will relate to each other and how built-in items, such as bookcases or fireplace mantles, will work together.

EXTERIOR ENTRY: We wanted to update the house while staying true to the original design.

MAKING A WISH LIST

A REMODELING WISH LIST can be as extensive as you need it to be. The more complete it is, the more likely you will avoid misunderstandings when work begins and the more likely you will be to end up with the results you want. Your wish list might include the following details:

Exterior

- Porch style and type
- Entry doors—shape and type
- Rooflines and angles
- Number of stories
- Roofing materials
- Window placement and/or features—dormers, skylights, casements
- Walkways
- Siding types—shingles, beveled board, stucco, brick
- Gardens and plantings
- Garage and access points
- Decks and balconies
- Other decorative features—deck railings, shutters, window boxes, trim

Interior: Layout

- Where you'll want privacy versus open space
- The flow of the rooms—from the front of the house to the back
- Stairwell access, hallway width, and storage spaces
- Amount of natural light
- Number and types of rooms—bedrooms, bathrooms, laundry room, closets
- Uses for each room. As you think about this category, try to envision your uses of the room. This will help you understand how important a room might be in the context of your lifestyle. When you begin working with an architect, you'll have a good feel for which rooms are critical and which rooms you might want to give up for budgetary or other reasons.
- Kitchen layout, appliances, and surfaces—bar, eating nook, countertop and cabinetry locations, appliance locations
- Bathroom layout and surfaces—tubs, toilets, sinks, mirrors, tile

Interior: Special Features

- Window/door styles and hardware
- Trim—for windows, doors, baseboard, crown molding, wainscoting
- Walls—smooth or rough; arched, square, or column doorway openings
- Fireplaces—configuration, types, surfaces
- Tiling
- Built-ins—window seats, bookcases, linen and coat closets, art nooks
- Stairs, railings, and banisters
- Storage spaces
- Ceiling height and structures (for instance, a vaulted ceiling for the master bedroom)
- Floor types—hardwood, tile, vinyl, cork, carpeting, concrete

- Lighting—such as spotlights, can lights, pendant, or sconce fixtures.
- Audio-video systems and cabling—Internet and phone ports, doorbell, security system, intercom, speakers, TV locations, and cable ports

The Power Plant

- Heating, venting, and air-conditioning (HVAC)
- Furnaces
- In-floor heating
- Hot-water tanks
- Air-conditioning
- Filtering and air-circulation systems
- Central vac
- Plumbing

The Design-Build Model

In order to successfully develop a working plan for your own renovation, it helps to understand the process the professionals use. This is known as the design-build model.

The design-build model is an approach that allocates the entire responsibility for design and construction to a single entity. In a traditional construction project led by a general contractor or builder, the process is called a Contractor-Led Design-Build. The contractor may do some of the work but will usually hire a designer and sub out electrical, plumbing, and the like.

When an architect or design firm assumes this role, the process is called a Design-Led Design-Build. In this case, the architect develops the design and prepares the construction drawings, then subs out all of the labor.

When you, the homeowner, take on the task of general contracting, it's reasonable to say your project is an Owner-Led Design-Build. In this case, you take responsibility for purchasing the materials and hiring the architect and all of the labor needed for the project.

Benefits to You. In addition to saving the fee you would normally pay a general contractor, you also eliminate any possible conflicts of interest. An unscrupulous contractor or designer can't take advantage of you by skimping on the design or materials and pocketing the profits.

The Disadvantages. The flip side of the arrangement is that the project leader—you, in this case—holds the ultimate responsibility for any losses, delays, or cost overruns. If there is a problem, it's your responsibility to find a solution.

The Juggling Act

The design-build process assumes parallel effort in several different areas and involves constant collaboration and cross-checking between the various people and companies working on the project. The goal is to make all of the separate functions that go into a major remodel work together within the allotted budget. For example, as a general contractor you may be working with an architect to finalize your blueprints while simultaneously researching framing companies, lumber or concrete suppli-

ers, and others to discuss the possibility of working with them. Construction takes time, but the fact that you're working on multiple fronts at the same time speeds the process and is one of the primary benefits of the design-build model.

Refining the Process. Another benefit of the Owner-Led Design-Build is that it provides you with the nimble ability to modify your project early on, making design changes or altering materials to keep costs down, all while maintaining the overall essence of your plan.

You'll be working with organizations and suppliers to determine which materials and methods will maximize your investment. When opportunities arise to obtain better quality materials or make slight improvements to the design, you can do so without having to re-bid the entire project. You'll simply incorporate the modification across all organizations.

The collaborative nature of this approach provides you with information and insight that you would not have if someone else were the general contractor. You will be able to react to problems quickly. And because you are in charge, there's little chance that you will overestimate the budget to line someone else's pockets. Being in the center of the action means that when an opportunity presents itself, you can take advantage of it.

> One of the biggest mistakes you can make is to take your remodeling project to an extreme, either by rushing in without a clear picture of the end game or by delaying the construction process because you are obsessing over every detail. The best approach is to remain flexible within the framework of your plan, taking advantage of opportunities as they arise.

Originally, we wanted a covered porch with French doors that lead to the great room. The covered porch didn't work out, but we love the new patio area, opposite.

CHAPTER 3

CONSTRUCTION DRAWINGS

- LEARN TO WORK WITH AN ARCHITECT OR DESIGNER TO CREATE YOUR CONSTRUCTION DRAWINGS

- SEE THE DIFFERENT TYPES OF DRAWINGS YOU WILL NEED FOR YOUR PROJECT

- CREATE YOUR OWN DRAWINGS

Hiring an Architect

Until now, we've been talking in generalities to help you determine if remodeling is right for you. But the generalities end here. If you are certain that a remodeling project is the right course of action, and you know what you need to make your project a success, it's time to refine your thoughts and put your ideas on paper.

The Design Process

Working with an architect is a creative process. A good architect will help you figure out what your remodel will cost, what it will look like, and how it will impact your existing home.

Different architects work in different ways. Some provide soup-to-nuts services, while others will offer their expertise by the hour. In general, it's only when a remodel involves the relocation or addition of new walls, rooms, or stairwells; adding an additional level; or changing the footprint of your home that an architect is necessary.

If you do not plan to keep your architect on a monthly retainer to oversee the construction work, set aside a small fund to pay for some hourly consulting. At the very minimum, have your architect come to the job site several times during the framing stage to make sure that your framing contractor doesn't miss anything.

There will also be situations requiring a new design solution that only an architect can provide.

Your architect's fees will include the cost of design and construction drawings, plus consulting expenses. To keep these costs to a minimum, tell your subcontractors that they need your permission before they call the architect with questions. Also, be sure to allow them to work out some problems themselves, especially if you hire talented professionals. When you empower these folks to take ownership and work in partnership, they will.

The most expensive words ever spoken by the home remodeler are, "While we're at it …"
—Pete Sandall, Sandall Norrie Architects

THE ARCHITECT'S ROLE

AN ARCHITECT will provide the following services:

- Develop initial schematic drawings that provide information on how new additions or levels will integrate with the existing structure.
- Draft a complete set of blueprints to be used by your local building department for issuing permits and by subcontractors for bidding and construction.

- Represent you during the building department review and approval process. The architect will work with the building department and other professionals as needed until your plans comply with building codes.
- Oversee construction by making sure that your subcontractors are building according to plan and that their workmanship is professional.
- Provide design alternatives if modifications become necessary once construction is underway.

FIRST MEETING AGENDA

THESE ARE SOME OF THE ISSUES you should cover during your first meeting:

- Explain what sort of exterior features you want.
- Present the clippings, notes, and sketches you have saved to help explain your vision.
- Discuss special interior features, such as bookcases, extra-wide hallways, new windows, or cabinetry.
- Mention your existing furniture and how you envision it in each room. For example, if you have an 8-foot table that you must include in the kitchen, you'll need to plan for it.
- Provide your architect with a written wish list. Be as specific as possible.

The First Meeting

You'll not only be interviewing one or more architects to see which one is the best fit for you, but they'll be assessing you as well. Be prepared to fully explain your ideas to your architect so that your initial meeting is productive and meaningful for both of you.

Naturally, you'll want to give the architect some idea of your budget, and—trust me—he will want to have that discussion with you, too. However, don't let your concerns about money get in the way of communicating what you truly want—at least during this early stage.

At the end of your first meeting, both you and the architect will decide if it makes sense to move to the next stage—the development of architectural plans.

MASTER BEDROOM: The master bedroom includes a gas fireplace insert surrounded by a custom-built mantle and a matching bookcase.

Now is the time to talk with a permit specialist in your local building department to determine which permits will be required for your project.

EVOLUTION OF THE EXTERIOR DESIGN

BECAUSE WE WANTED more living space, we decided to expand the main level and add a new second level. The new level would of course alter the exterior look of the house, but we wanted to retain the authentic feel of the 1925 bungalow that I fell in love with originally, including the turret around the front door. When working with an architect, you will find that any changes you make to the interior layout affect how the exterior will look. The drawings below show how the design progressed. After a series of meetings, discussions, and compromises, our architect, Pete Sandall, arrived at the drawing in the box, bottom right.

Architectural Plans

Architectural plans are developed in two phases. In phase one, you'll explore design options and compare costs. In phase two, you'll formalize your design with accurate, to-scale drawings that show the details necessary for the building department to approve your project and issue permits.

Phase One: Schematic Drawings

Schematics are simple ⅛-inch scale drawings that illustrate a variety of different floor plans, elevations, and perspectives. Expect to pay $1,500 to $2,500 for these drawings.

Schematics allow you to explore a variety of options for modifying both your exterior and interior layout. With each drawing, rooms will come and go, stairs or bathrooms can move from the front of the home to the back, and the exterior look of the house may drastically change.

Expect to see several rounds of schematics before you find a plan that you're excited about and that fits your budget.

Keep in mind that current average remodeling costs can range anywhere between $100–$400 per square foot, depending upon the work involved, how the job is managed, and the quality of materials used.

The cost estimates your architect provides for each design option generally reflect the use of standard building materials and the hiring of a general contractor as part of the project. However, as your own general contractor, you can safely assume that those costs can be reduced by as much as 40 percent.

> The architect's job is to blend your dreams with reality, with an eye toward efficiency and cost. That usually translates into a somewhat different version of your initial plan.

Learning Curve

The Architect's Job

We told our architect that we wanted to extend the back of the house by 20 to 25 feet. He returned a few days later with a highly efficient and affordable schematic that extended the house by just 9 feet. As we reviewed this plan, I secretly wondered if I had chosen the right architect and considered moving on to someone else. That was a natural—but unwise—instinct. Remember: the architect's job, and his primary value to you, is the ability to render your dreams in the most efficient, cost-effective way possible. The last thing that you or your architect wants to create is a plan that can't be executed because it is too expensive.

LAUNDRY ROOM   BATHROOM   FRONT ENTRY

GREAT ROOM

DECK

DOWN   UP

LIVING ROOM

KITCHEN

MAIN FLOOR PRELIMINARY DRAWING

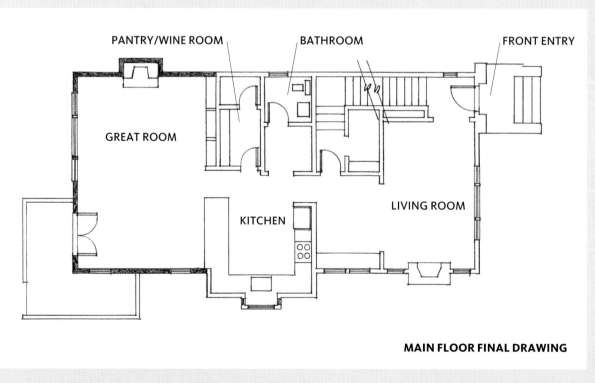

PANTRY/WINE ROOM   BATHROOM   FRONT ENTRY

GREAT ROOM

KITCHEN

LIVING ROOM

MAIN FLOOR FINAL DRAWING

CHOOSE YOUR ARCHITECT CAREFULLY because you will be working closely with them. When it comes to selecting an architect, the ability to listen to your ideas, communicate effectively, and be a pleasure to work with may be almost as important as design talent.

The floor plan shown opposite top is just one of many preliminary designs we viewed. The others are the final floor plans for the main, new second, and basement levels. In the end, we were able to incorporate those elements that were most important to us while maintaining the character of the home.

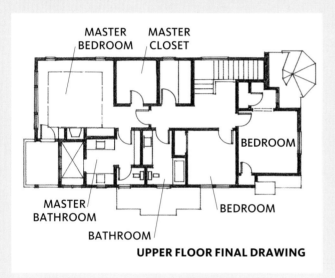

UPPER FLOOR FINAL DRAWING

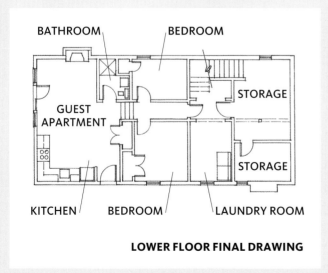

LOWER FLOOR FINAL DRAWING

Phase Two: Final Drawings

In this phase, the architect will develop ¼-inch scale drawings that illustrate exact dimensions and provide detailed notes on construction and materials, as well as placement of windows, doors, cabinetry, and other fixtures. These drawings will cost about 10 to 12 percent of your estimated remodeling budget.

This final set of permit drawings, or blueprints, also incorporates local building codes, land-use requirements, and other important information so that permits can be issued and construction will be in compliance with local building codes.

In addition to the master building permit, there are specific permits for plumbing, electrical, and heating and air conditioning that must be acquired through a licensed, in-state subcontractor.

For a significant remodel, a standard set of permit drawings might include:

A site plan that includes the location of existing structures and physical features of your property, plus any new additions and modifications.

A foundation plan that shows the dimensions of the foundation plus any changes or additions.

A floor plan that illustrates proposed changes to the interior space of your home.

A framing plan that identifies the size, spacing, and direction of all floor and ceiling joists, rafters, supporting walls, beams, and columns and illustrates how these will be connected to the new framing.

A structural wall section that shows a cross-section through a wall from the foundation to the roof. This plan is typically needed when changes are proposed within a wall or roof.

Building elevations that represent the exterior sides of your house. These are generally required when you plan to extend your home beyond the existing footprint.

A glazing and door schedule that lists the product type, size, and U-factor of each window and door.

Drawing Your Own Plans

If your project is a small one, such as replacing existing cabinetry or resurfacing a floor, you may be able to use your own drawings, or those prepared by a vendor, to manage the job yourself. (See "Do-It-Yourself Plans," below.)

It is important that your drawings contain accurate measurements. It is equally important that you understand the impact of each change you plan to make. Whenever possible, have the vendor come to your home and take their own measurements as part of the bidding process. Many local suppliers will actually come to your

Standard dimensions for kitchen cabinets have changed over the years, so you may not be able to simply replace or add new cabinets without having to repair or upgrade other parts of an older kitchen—such as flooring or countertops.

home, make suggestions, and then provide a drawing with the proposed layout at no cost.

Your drawing should include all of the room measurements along with the location and measurements of the existing fixtures, appliances, and installed features. When you work from your own plans, you will be using the existing room fixtures and configuration as a basis for discussion of remodeling options with various vendors. These discussions will allow you to consider small-impact options, such as replacing an older sink or appliance with a new one, as well as add-on options, such as new lighting, which will require the services of an electrician.

If you like drawing and are comfortable on the computer, you can also try your hand at using one of the free online software programs that allow you to draw 3D models of anything you like.

In addition to drawings, you should also take "before" pictures of the rooms you plan to remodel to use in your discussions, as they may identify a problem area or concern that you, as an inexperienced homeowner, might not initially see or recognize.

Learning Curve

A Preemptive Decision

The Land Use Department notified me that my property might have a methane-gas problem. The geological engineer I hired told me I could either test for methane or proceed with having mitigation techniques installed. I chose the latter, which consisted of covering the ground with plastic sheeting and purchasing special sleeves for the plumbing pipes that would go through the foundation. A geological engineer then inspected the area prior to the pouring of the foundation.

This is a perfect example of an unexpected and unforeseen expense—but one I would have had regardless of whether I was managing my remodel project or not. Why did I choose to assume that methane was present and hire the engineering firm? Because if it was, I would have doubled my expense by paying for the test as well as the mitigation cost.

Other Professionals

Surveyors. If your remodel expands the footprint of your home, a land survey is sometimes required when there is a property line concern, or elevation is an issue. The survey will provide the exact boundaries of your property. Occasionally, a survey is also required to secure the building permit. If a survey is requested, find out who wants it, and why.

Engineers. Your architect will typically bring in a professional structural engineer to provide gravity, stress, and load calculations when needed. If you're not using an architect, you may still need to hire a structural engineer. Some of the tasks that require an engineer include moving walls, enlarging or adding windows or staircases, and dealing with existing problem areas, such as sloping floors, cracked plaster, and other signs of structural weakness. It's better to invest the $500 in structural engineering than to lose thousands later to make repairs.

If your home is in good condition prior to construction, assume that the basic strength and integrity of your building is fine, and engineering will only be required on those portions of the house affected by your remodel plan. If you're planning a large remodel, include a budget of approximately 1–1½ percent of the cost of the new construction to cover this expense.

Changes during construction, even time-saving ideas suggested by your professional construction team, can lead to additional structural engineering costs.

Engineering Old Houses. If you have an older, stick-framed home, structural engineering can be complicated because you cannot use basic load-calculation formulas. In order to get your remodeling plan approved for this type of home, you might need to add support structures, such as beams, and additional sheathing and shingling to achieve a stable structure. As you can imagine, this would definitely increase the cost of your remodel.

Use of heavy finish materials may require the installation of additional support structures.

FAMILY ROOM: We told the architect that we loved books and we wanted built-ins to display them.

Environmental Engineering. You may require additional engineering advice when the building department reviews your plans, or sometimes when construction itself begins. For example, if your project affects a lake or stream or there are grading issues, you may need to consult a civil engineer. Water table or gas issues, such as methane or radon, might require environmental testing and engineering followed by remedial action. The engineer can specify the type of work required to solve each problem. There's nothing to be done on the front end to prevent this except to understand that it's a possibility and set aside funds in the event a problem occurs.

Interior Designer. Up until recently, most homeowners considered the use of an interior designer a luxury that only the wealthy could afford. Today's homeowner can tap into the invaluable services of a design professional, thanks to an expansion in the field and a wide array of high-quality materials available at a lower cost.

Unlike an interior decorator, an interior designer develops the functionality, design, and overall look and feel of an interior space.

An interior designer's job is to work with you to define your needs and style and then create an interior design plan. These drawings will indicate how the space will be modified, what specific materials will be used, and what elements—such as fireplaces, bookshelves, and lighting—will be installed. Interior designers have a broad range of knowledge in the areas of electrical capacity, safety, and construction, as well as a talent for designing and implementing aesthetically pleasing, functional spaces. While interior designers frequently work in partnership with architects, they can be used as a stand-alone resource for smaller remodeling projects. They can provide insight and experience to help you not only develop a plan and figure out what materials to use, but also to execute the plan. Like architects, interior designers can oversee construction along with you to ensure that your project proceeds according to plan.

Obtaining Permits

Your architect can file your plans with the local land-use office and in the process answer any questions they may have. However, a large project usually requires several permits. There is one "master" building permit, which you will get through the filing of your plans; however, depending upon the extent of your remodel, other permits for specific work may include:

- Plumbing
- Heating
- Sewer
- Electrical

Some of these permits, such as heating and air conditioning, may be acquired only through a licensed, in-state subcontractor. You can file for the others yourself. As long as you have the work properly inspected and approved, you can hire whomever you like to do the job.

The permitting process will educate you about building requirements and other compliance concerns, such as utility upgrades, that will be required for your remodel.

One benefit of adding the second level and the extra bedrooms is that it allowed me to turn one of them into an office, opposite.

CHAPTER 4

ASSEMBLING YOUR TEAM

The Do-Ability Test

Armed with your architect's working drawings, you're ready to take the next big step.
It is now time to test both your ability to manage your own project and to find out whether
the plans you have on paper can actually be built. In this phase you'll discover

- Your skills at multitasking, organizing, and making quick decisions.
- Whether you can find and hire the people you need.
- Your ability to secure the necessary financing.

Don't be surprised if you feel a bit uneasy during this phase. The tasks ahead of you are formidable and will actually require more time and energy than anything that happens once construction begins.

YOUR ROLE AS THE HGC

AS THE HGC (Homeowner General Contractor), you're about to take on a job that will require lots of attention to details, collaborating with subcontractors and vendors, making decisions, scheduling, and managing people. If you haven't figured out how you're going to fit all of this in with your usual responsibilities, now is the time to start preparing.

To begin, here is a brief list of what you can reasonably expect if you manage your own remodel:

- You will make multiple phone calls to get one thing done.

- You will sometimes be frustrated or scared by your lack of knowledge.

- You will be required to learn a few things as you go along.

- You will have to baby-sit others to keep your project running smoothly and on time.

- It will always be your responsibility to make sure that all of the "wrongs" are turned into "rights."

- You will make mistakes, but you will rely on the expertise of your team to help you recover.

- There will be discrepancies between your design plan and your eventual outcome.

- You can—and will—do your job right, and your remodel will turn out well.

Getting Organized

No one can successfully manage a complex, costly effort by keeping all the facts and figures in their head. For the HGC, that translates into a few simple tools:

- Portable filing boxes
- Resource notebook (to hold contact information)
- Fax capability

There will be many situations in which you'll need to consult your records while you're on the fly. Having a portable filing system not only will help you do your job but will help everyone else do his or her job. Your workers will quickly realize that they can count on you for access to the information or contact numbers they need.

I suggest you buy two lightweight, accordion-style file boxes to use as your portable office. Label one the "Design File Box," and the other the "Contractor File Box." Each will have a very different function.

Resource Notebook

Buy yourself a small notebook to record your contact names and numbers. Carry it with you wherever you go. As you manage your project, you'll find yourself reaching for this information in the car, at work, and everywhere in between. By the time my own remodel was complete, I had more than 170 different vendors, contractors, and company phone numbers in my notebook—from concrete cutters and tile suppliers to wrought-iron railing manufacturers and engineers. Every time you meet with

Whenever you can, capture and record multiple vendors or subcontractor's names and numbers. This will provide you with alternative resources in case of an emergency.

DESIGN FILE BOX

THIS FILE WILL HELP YOU keep track of *design elements,* such as flooring and surfaces, room layouts, built-ins, and other such details. Keep the photos you've taken of architectural features you like, as well as pictures you've cut out of magazines. Your design file will also contain *product and style information,* including appliance measurements, paint chips, tile samples, carpet swatches, and the like.

The box will probably contain more information on products than you will use in your design. In the beginning, you will be constantly adding and discarding materials as you change your mind, find something better, or reject an idea completely because your priorities have changed.

Your design file will serve two very important purposes. First, it will help you explain what you want to your subcontractors. Second, the samples will provide visual, specific information while you're on the job site. For example, when your framer is building the walls of your kitchen, you'll have the exact measurements of your new refrigerator at hand.

Divide your design file by rooms or materials, depending on your project. For example, your kitchen section will hold comprehensive information on appliances and fixtures, flooring, cabinetry, and countertops.

Sample Design File Labels

- Bedrooms
- Bathrooms
- Furniture
- Lighting
- Window Coverings
- Kitchen
- Appliances
- Flooring
- Fireplaces
- Cabinetry

THE CONTRACTOR FILE BOX will hold contracts and bids, lien releases, the master schedule, the budget, architect plans, building permits, and other working documents. You will also use it to hold receipts and delivery information. You will need this data every time you discuss work with your subcontractors.

Having your business files with you also allows you to make use of the wait time you'll inevitably have while you're on the job site. Finally, if you're having a disagreement with a particular subcontractor about promised work, a quick look at the original contract can solve the dispute.

Sample Contractor File Labels

- Windows
- Roof
- Siding
- Framing
- Insulation
- Electrical
- HVAC
- Finish Carpentry
- Cabinets
- Doors
- Gutters
- Deck
- Lumber
- Drywall
- Plumbing
- Painting
- Tile
- Fabrication
- Concrete (foundation and flat work)

a new subcontractor, or get a professional recommendation, write it down, or staple their business card to one of the blank pages.

As your project nears completion, move your paint chips and swatches into your resource notebook. It is easier to carry the book than the accordion file as you go on shopping expeditions.

Get a Fax. Despite the technology revolution, many contractors do not use email or the Internet as part of their business. The fax machine remains an important communication tool in the construction world. Save yourself time and effort by adding a fax line to your home telephone service.

Always keep your file boxes and plans with you.
You never know when you will need them.

Shopping Around

It's now time to start shopping. This is a multistage expedition. First, you will gather your working drawings and your design file to help you "shop" for the right people for your job. The first step is to create a detailed shopping list of all the items and materials you will need to purchase.

> You'll get more respect when you visit job sites if bring along your working plans. Some professionals won't even talk to you unless you can show them solid evidence that you mean business.

Your working drawings will help you create this list of materials, fixtures, and appliances. The list will help you determine which types of subcontractors you will need to hire. Here are suggestions for organizing your list.

1. **Create a list of all materials and products needed, including quantities, to complete each room in your plan.** For example, in your new master bathroom you'll need new floor and wall tile, two new sinks, two new faucets, two mirrors, a remote-operating skylight, one toilet paper holder, one glass shower door, and the like. Be sure your list includes everything—right down to the new pipes and wiring needed.

2. **Categorize according to subcontractor.** Categorize the items according to the subcontractor who will perform the work. This will help you to develop specific summaries of tasks and materials so that you can request bids and draw up contracts. You can create one of these for each room or major area in your project.

3. **Develop your shopping list.** Divide the list into those products you will supply and those your contractor will provide.

LABOR & MATERIALS LISTS

A SUBCONTRACTOR TASK AND MATERIALS LIST for a master bathroom might look like this:

Plumber
Tasks
1. Install 2 sinks with fixtures
2. Install 1 toilet
3. Install shower fixtures
4. Install new sewage line and tie into existing line
5. Add new plumbing lines to master bath and tie into existing plumbing

Materials
1. Copper piping (plumber)
2. PVC sewer line (plumber)
3. 2 sink faucets (homeowner)
4. Shower faucets and fixtures (homeowner)
5. Sinks, toilet (homeowner)

Of course, this is only a partial list. For a typical master bath remodel you may also require lists for carpenters, drywall contractors, tile setters, countertop fabricators, and the like.

You'll also want to make a multiroom requirements list for certain contractors, which might look something like this:

Drywaller
1. Master bath
2. Master bedroom with vaulted ceiling
3. Kitchen
4. New stairway to end of hall

A list similar to the "Labor and Materials Lists" above resulted in this master bathroom, opposite.

Finding Your Partners

How do you actually find high-quality, well-respected contractors and suppliers? It takes more than letting your fingers do the walking through the local Yellow Pages. The best professionals may not advertise at all because good word-of-mouth keeps them busy.

Approach your search from a different angle. Contact your local Master Builders Association to get complete listings of tradesmen in your area. You can also call plumbing wholesalers, masonry wholesalers, and similar suppliers to ask for references. It's likely that they can provide you with a list of established professionals with whom they regularly do business.

Another tactic is to case your neighborhood or a nearby area that has active construction projects. Notice who's remodeling or building; stop by the job site; and in-troduce yourself to the subcontractors. If they regularly work for one general contractor, find out whether they do side jobs. If so, give them your phone number. You'd be surprised at how many will call you about extra work once they're off the clock. Many of them operate their own businesses, carry full insurance, and charge less than the general contractor would for the same work.

Understanding the Trades. There are a surprising number of specialties in the construction industry. There are experts who do nothing but jack-up houses or pour

Follow the HGC mantra: hire the right subcontractor for the right job.

The best way to find high-quality workers is through recommendations from building associations and suppliers, opposite.

Many subcontractors who primarily work with one general contractor are eager to pick up side jobs "off the clock," above.

foundations or cut concrete. There are artisans who hone and install granite countertops, others who will spray-paint your entire home without a single drip.

Danger Sign. Occasionally, you might encounter a tradesman who claims to be good at everything, from painting to cabinetry to plumbing. If you're a first-timer, this can seem like a fabulous deal. It's not.

The reality is that most subcontractors are no better than you at performing a job outside their area of expertise. It's also unlikely that they will have the proper tools for a wide range of construction tasks.

One of the biggest mistakes you can make is to single-source your project to one professional claiming universal talent and skill. What will happen is one of two things: they'll end up subcontracting out part of the work to their brother-in-law, or—worse—they'll do a poor job all by themselves.

This does not mean that you must hire an army of super-specialists. In certain cases, you can leverage the skills of a particular subcontractor to save time and money. For example, you might find a plumbing company that will also take on your sewer work, which eliminates the need to hire a sewer professional. This only works if you use experienced, licensed, insured, and bonded professionals with expertise in a crossover area. They're not likely to risk their reputation and business by taking on tasks they can't do well.

ONCE YOU COMPLETE YOUR SHOPPING AND LIST MAKING, you'll be more equipped to assess how specific features of your design impact your budget. For instance, if you've planned for heated floors in your master bath, you've jotted down the approximate cost of installation and priced the systems you like. Suddenly, you realize that this feature will add around $6,000 to the cost of your master bath. It's now time to decide whether

- **Your budget is large enough to include this feature, OR**

- **You can reduce costs elsewhere, OR**

- **You'd rather use the money in another area of the remodel.**

As you talk with subcontractors, you'll also begin to see a few gaps in your plan that require extra materials or labor. As you identify them, add them to your list and update your project costs. Sometimes, what seems like a small change—such as deciding to buy a different type of kitchen faucet—can have a surprisingly large impact on your subcontractor's labor and materials costs. Keep your team in the loop on any changes you make in your design. The more details you are able to provide, the closer their bids will be to the actual cost.

Another benefit of your detailed list making is that when you invite subcontractors to bid on your job, each one is getting the identical information about what you want done. Later, when they submit their bids, their estimates should be much closer to what the job will actually cost.

A good contractor can suggest enhancements to your original plans. For example, a tile setter may recommend glass-tile insets for the face of a neutral mantle.

Work Your Plans

Despite your architect's best efforts, his or her drawings will not contain all the information your contractors will need.

Unlike commercial construction—which typically includes mechanical and electrical design on the blueprints—your residential plans probably provide only the structural details, such as the framing of walls, floors, roof, and foundation. Issues such as plumbing, heating, and air conditioning are usually determined during construction.

Typically, the architect will allocate a standard amount of space for the fixtures, allowing for some wiggle room within the design. However, it's important to have a clearer idea of where things will be routed during this early phase. This is because ducts and pipes can affect your layout and wall and ceiling heights, and can even create noise concerns (such as hearing the upstairs toilet flushing in the kitchen). You'll also need this information to ensure that the contract with your framer includes whatever is required to support these mechanical and electrical infrastructures.

As the HGC, you'll need to work one-on-one with the plumber, the furnace installer, and other subcontractors to determine how each system will be installed, what is needed to support it, and how it will integrate with the rest of your system.

Take a Meeting. Start by setting up individual meetings at the job site with two or three mechanical and electrical subcontractors. (Save time by scheduling them one to two hours apart on the same day.)

A good subcontractor will tour the home and—this is important—ask questions to find out how your existing systems are set up and what needs to change to accommodate your remodel plan. If no questions are asked, this is not a subcontractor for you!

Expect each subcontractor to offer options and even pencil in ideas on your drawings. Compare these notes with the other contractors you meet to determine which plan is the most workable with the other systems in your home. In the process, you will also get a sense of the skills and knowledge of the subcontractors you meet.

Learning Curve

Did I Forget Anything?

Trust me, every homeowner who remodels is blind. I say this with all due respect because it was true for me, and at some point in your own project, the same will be true for you.

Despite going over construction plans countless times, and knowing full well that my project involved a complete tear-down of almost everything inside the house, I simply did not include the cost of demolition in my project. I had this silly notion that demolition was something that I could do by myself over a weekend. You know, bring in a few trash bags and a sledgehammer and go at it.

It wasn't until I saw the worry unfold on the faces of my framer and concrete contractor that I began to understand that demolition is by no means a simple, one-shot deal. While you're tearing out the foundation wall, you need to prop up the back of the house with beams. If you remove the roof too soon, you can destabilize your entire house.

In a large remodel, demolition is an intricate, multistage process that the subcontractors work out in partnership. I now understand the magnitude of that effort. Not exactly a small weekend project.

Don't leave out the cost of demolition as I did. Believe me, it is a lot harder than it looks to do it right.

The Bidding Process

The most important part of the bidding process is making sure that the subcontractors you select to bid on your project are experienced, licensed, and insured professionals. In fact, one of the most common mistakes homeowners make is that they don't thoroughly research their subcontractors before they hire them.

Like any other business, the construction industry has its share of shady characters and *faux* experts. Don't be lured into hiring someone solely on price or personality. Neither of these qualities will help your project pass inspection, especially if the work is subpar.

You also want to choose suppliers who are willing and able to correct something when it goes wrong. Expect that there will be problems, and know that recourse is only available if you use a professional.

Get Multiple Bids. As noted earlier, get three separate bids from three different contractors for each piece of your project. The best way to know whether you're getting a good deal is to compare one set of qualifications, services, and materials against another.

After you've talked with a subcontractor about your project and shown him your home, you're ready to solicit a formal request for a bid. This can be done in person at the time of your meeting or by mail. In either case, you want to clarify a general timeframe for the project and supply them with all the information applicable to their portion of the work. Request a line-item bid in order to collect as much information as possible.

Most subcontractors will need a copy of your blueprints in order to develop a complete bid. Make 10 to 20 additional copies of your plans so that you can give one to each of the contractors.

A good subcontractor will be able to properly estimate the amount of work your project will take and provide you with a fixed price that accurately reflects the labor and time required.

Learn from the Bids. Once you receive your bids, use them to evaluate the work that is required for your project. For example, if one contractor puts an item in a bid but another one doesn't, find out why. Do you really need the extra item? Go back to each contractor, and ask them to explain the thinking behind their bid. You may find that you don't need the extra item, or you may learn that the item is important. In any case, your questions will show that you are serious and know what you want. This is likely to prompt discussions and new information that will lead to a more successful project.

DO YOUR HOMEWORK

- **Contact your state's department of labor** to find out whether the subcontractor has a current business license and any outstanding liens. You may also be able to check the company's on-the-job injury stats and find out whether they owe any worker's compensation taxes.

- **Contact your local Master Building Association** to check whether the contractor is a member.

- **Call the Better Business Bureau** to learn whether it has received complaints about the contractor.

- **Ask for references from previous clients.**

- **Consider it a red flag** if there are long gaps between your contractor's jobs. A good contractor typically has a backlog of projects.

- **Look at the contractor's work.** Many people skip this step, but it provides the most accurate picture of how your own work will be accomplished.

Your conversations with subcontractors and the bids they deliver will help you understand the scope of work each one handles. You might realize that there are additional tradespeople you will need to hire. You will also get some idea of the sequence of the tasks that go into your project. This is critical because, as the HGC, you need to be sure you have someone lined up for every single component of the work in order to stay on schedule and keep your subcontractors onsite and productive.

While you are processing all this information, it will become clear which contractor is best able to handle your project. The final choice seems to happen naturally as you compare labor costs, expertise, and suggested approaches.

A walkway runs alongside the house from the front gate to the detached garage. The garage is the building in the background, at the far end of the path.

Learning Curve

"Saved By an Angel"

That sentiment takes on a whole new meaning when you find a skilled subcontractor who is willing to offer you some help when you need it most.

When I began my project, I thought that anyone with the job title "concrete subcontractor" would naturally be able to create anything out of cement—including fountains and nymph statues. In reality, the person who sets and pours your concrete foundation footings may not have the expertise to pour your walls, floors, or driveway.

There are many trade professionals who specialize in one type of work and nothing else. Typically, it is the job of the general contractor to hire the individual subcontractors for each step. But when the general contractor is you, it's great to have a knowledgeable pro around to offer you some guidance.

In addition to the foundation and flat work he provided, my concrete subcontractor agreed to oversee excavation and house support during demolition. Thanks to that agreement, I had a skilled manager direct one of the most critical areas of my construction. Sure, I paid more for the privilege, but it saved me considerable work and provided me with the piece of mind that comes with being covered under someone else's insurance, warranty, and quality umbrella. With that kind of coverage, let it rain!

Some subcontractors will suggest performing the work on a "time and material" basis. **Don't do it.** This is a recipe for problems because you have no idea in advance how much of your time and budget will be required.

BASEMENT APARTMENT: We have four fireplaces in the house, but we wanted them all to be different. The floral tiles were reclaimed from a home built in the early part of the last century.

DRAWING UP CONTRACTS

MANY HOMEOWNERS simply accept a bid and begin work. This may be fine for an incidental repair project, but it's not a good approach for a homeowner managing multiple contractors. Without a contract, you have no way to establish your terms, conditions, and expectations.

Contracts will be covered in much greater detail in Chapter 5, but the process for developing them is simple:

- Thoroughly review the bid with the subcontractor to make sure you understand exactly what their work will include.
- Once you approve the bid, draft a contract containing the bid information and the terms you want to include.
- Plan on a few rounds of revisions before both of you are satisfied.
- Both parties sign the contract, and you provide the subcontractor with a signed copy.

The Art of Negotiation

In the world of construction, everything is negotiable—until the contract is signed.

Becoming a good negotiator requires courage and diplomacy. In other words, don't be afraid to ask questions, and be willing to compromise so that you can come to a mutually beneficial agreement. Negotiation means to deal or bargain with another, but it also means to navigate around obstacles in a satisfactory manner. You will sometimes find that the person across the table from you is the obstacle that needs your attention.

As the HGC, it's in your best interest to negotiate as much as you can while you're still in the bidding phase. For example, the tile installer you'd like to work with typically purchases the materials needed for the job. You have the opportunity to obtain exactly what you want at a cheaper price. Tell this contractor that you will be supplying the materials, and ask him to reduce his bid to reflect this. The same holds true for a small "extra" task you'd like a contractor to perform at no charge, as a means of securing your agreement to work with him. Study every aspect of your project to determine how you can eliminate, limit, or better control your costs.

Finally, don't confuse bids with contracts. Once you accept a subcontractor's bid, you still need to create a contract that incorporates his bid with your own terms.

IMPACT OF BIDS ON YOUR DESIGN BUDGET

AT SOME POINT IN THE BIDDING PROCESS—even before all the final bids are delivered—you'll develop a fairly good idea of what it will cost to execute your working plans exactly as they were rendered. For example, after speaking with flooring installers, you'll learn that it typically costs anywhere from $6 to $7.50 per square foot to install hardwood flooring. Using the square footage listed on your plans, you'll be able to calculate an assumed cost (plus tax) for this section of the work.

Is this more than you planned to spend on this portion of your project? If you'd like to tweak anything, now is the time. You can save money by making your changes on paper instead of in the field. Once you know the cost of completing a particular facet of your project, ask your architect to rework the design to stay within your budget.

Establishing a Budget

There is no way to know how well you are managing the cost of your project unless you've first established a budget. This will keep you on track and provide you with the power for both restraint and permission.

What you actually spend on a component of the job versus what you originally budgeted for it isn't nearly as important as your ability to balance losses and gains across the board. So, when windows end up costing $3,000 more than you expected, you'll be able to look at your budget and find another area where costs can be trimmed to make up the difference.

Fixed versus Flexible Expenses. There are certain non-negotiable expenses that you'll be required to pay in order to finalize your project. Because you'll have little control over these costs, don't waste time trying to reduce them. Architectural plans are one example. As discussed, these can range from 5 to 15 percent of the total cost of your project. In addition, you'll have to pay permit expenses, as well as any other engineering or survey fees associated with getting an approved set of working drawings.

The mantel and bookcase in the master bedroom were crafted from African mahogany and were well worth the extra cost.

Living Expenses. If you choose to move off-site during construction, you will need to budget for the expense. Understand that a large remodel project will not only disrupt your normal life but force you to incur additional living expenses, such as the cost of a temporary residence. If this is the case, you'll also need to factor in the following:

- The cost of moving and monthly storage for furnishings, fixtures, vehicles, and pets.

- The cost of packing and moving personal effects and basic household items into temporary housing.

- Monthly housing, food, and utilities (budget for an additional 45 days to accommodate schedule changes).

- The cost of moving household items and family back into your home.

If you stay in the house, assume that you will occasionally eat meals out, bathe elsewhere, and invest in off-site storage for household goods. At the very least, you'll need to buy plenty of plastic sheeting and duct tape!

> If you are tempted to save a few bucks by doing the demolition yourself, remember: *Every day you spend taking apart your home is a day that you could be building.*

Deciding to completely move out of your home during a remodel can be an epic undertaking. Don't add to the time, effort, cost, and chaos by making it a last-minute decision.

Destruction Has Its Price. In the excitement of planning your remodel, it's easy to forget that you first have to remove what you don't want. In some older homes especially, demolition might uncover hazardous materials, such as asbestos or lead paint. These will require professional removal and disposal at an extra cost. There may be structural issues that will require a demolition crew to build temporary stabilizing structures to keep your home from collapsing. You may need to demolish in stages, as different areas of your home are torn apart and then rebuilt.

Hire professionals who can complete your demolition quickly and efficiently, and insist that your demolition subcontractor add you as an additional insured on their company insurance policy.

Expert demolition contractors can take a house apart without causing damage to the areas that will remain. Here the old siding was stripped away before the outside wall and foundation were removed for the new addition.

THINK GREEN: TURN YOUR TRASH INTO TREASURE

BY REUSING OR RESELLING materials that would otherwise be discarded during your demolition, you not only help the environment, but you can save or even earn money. Faucets, sinks, toilets, towel racks, mirrors, cabinets, hardware, and lighting fixtures can be reused or sold at a yard sale, at a consignment store, or on the Internet.

The most valuable items for the secondary market are antique faucets, sinks, clawfoot tubs, and door hardware. An item in good condition in any of these categories could fetch several hundred dollars.

Discarded wood flooring, shutters, siding, windows, doors, and tile may also be salvaged, but you must decide whether the reward would justify the effort. For instance, hardwood flooring must be carefully disassembled in long pieces with all the nails removed. Cherry-pick the easiest, most valuable items, and then remove them for reuse or resale.

Anything you can sell will improve your bottom line and keep the materials out of the waste stream. Some materials that you can't sell can still be recycled or donated. Check with your local building department for resources.

Don't forget about the small visual details, such as this charming wall fountain, which help bring life to a home.

Landscaping is one area that is often overlooked when drawing up a budget for a major remodel, opposite.

Costs for Materials. Use the shopping list of materials discussed earlier in this chapter to complete the materials portion of your budget. Finalize the price for those items you definitely plan to purchase, and establish "placeholder" costs for materials you may later need.

Don't forget to factor in sales tax and the cost of delivery or off-site storage where applicable. These can add up fast on a large remodel project.

Cost Planning Tip. In order to be sure you've covered all your bases, refer to Chapter 6, "A Building Overview," to get an idea of the labor and materials needed for each phase of construction. Then set up an assumed cost for each category of work included in your project based on your bids and your materials costs.

The Slush Fund. While your bids will cover most of the work to be done, it's inevitable that one or more tasks will come up that will require extra materials or manpower. In addition, there are construction costs that are so incidental that the novice can easily ignore them—until they add up. Extra electricity to support power tool usage, the monthly cost of a portable toilet, and incidental laborers for site cleanup are just a few examples.

There's also the possibility that raw construction materials may suddenly skyrocket, as they did by nearly 20 percent in the wake of Hurricane Katrina. A disaster drives costs up because inventories of materials are depleted quickly and goods become scarce.

Put the money you will use for your project into a checking or savings account that is dedicated to your project. Commingling your remodel funds with your household money will make it difficult to manage and track your expenses.

IF YOU HAVE EQUITY built up in your home, you are current on your mortgage payments, and you have good credit, you probably assume that you can easily obtain financing for your project. Not necessarily.

In today's economic climate, many lenders are hesitant to offer a construction loan for a renovation project that the homeowner plans to oversee. As a result, it is unlikely that you can get a loan based on the enhanced value of your home post-remodel. However, there are several other approaches that you can use to fund your project. Just be sure to have the financing in place before demolition starts.

Home equity loans are available for anywhere from 65 to 85 percent of the current value of the home. To qualify, you'll need full documentation of your income, a professional appraisal, and great credit. Typically, equity lines of credit have minimal fees, so they're the cheapest way to secure funds.

There is no limitation on how you use the money and no bank involvement in your construction project.

The downside is that interest rates on home equity lines of credit are often higher than a mortgage and carry a variable interest rate. And unlike a 30-year fixed-rate mortgage, the repayment terms vary.

A **cash-out refinance** assumes you'll refinance the entire value of your home, and withdraw the equity value (again 65 to 85 percent of the current market value of the home) to complete your project. This is a particularly good option if interest rates are low.

With a **second mortgage,** you maintain your current mortgage, and find a different lender to loan you the difference between what the home is worth minus the debt on the first loan. You will also have to maintain your bank's minimum equity value in the home. Like the home equity loan, there are no strings attached to how or where you use the money.

Creating Schedules

Based on your discussions with everyone involved, you have a general idea of how long your project is going to take and who will be doing what. It's now time to build your construction schedule.

The Master Schedule. This should include

- Subcontractor work schedules, tasks, and time lines.
- Preliminary delivery dates for materials and appliances.
- Holidays and weekends.

Putting your project down on a simple calendar will provide you with an estimated completion date. Workers and suppliers will repeatedly ask you for this date to gauge how much wiggle room they might have. Circle your completion date in red on your calendar, and stick to it—a deadline is a powerful motivator.

Building Permit Schedule. When you set a start date for your remodel, plan for more than one round of reviews by your local building department. If permits come in earlier, that's even better. If not, your contractors won't be derailed by any delays.

Subcontractor Schedules. It's imperative that the subcontractor contracts include a basic time line that has been developed in partnership with each sub so that you can schedule other subcontractors before and after them. This also keeps your subcontractors motivated.

Dealing with the Weather

If your project involves work on exterior walls, foundation, or roof, assume that weather may delay your schedule. The best way to handle that, along with any over-optimistic time lines provided by your subcontractors, is to build a few extra days into every single phase of your project. For instance, if your plumber assumes 10 days for his work, build 12 days into your schedule.

DO YOU PASS THE DO-ABILITY TEST?

YOU ARE FULLY PREPARED TO MOVE FORWARD IF

- You've confirmed the interest and availability of your subcontractors.

- Received and approved all bids from your subcontractors.

- Talked with suppliers and researched materials, costs, and delivery time lines.

- Worked with your architect on any necessary modifications to your plans.

- Submitted your plans to the building department for any final changes prior to receiving your permits.

GARAGE: We wanted a detached garage near the back of the property. We saved a little by reusing the old windows from the living room on the garage.

Stuff happens. Be sure to include a few extra days in your schedule to allow for unexpected circumstances such as bouts of nasty weather.

CHAPTER 5

PREPARING FOR CONSTRUCTION

Cramping Your Style?

One of the biggest decisions you'll make about your remodel is how you're going to live through it. If you plan on staying in your home, expect to lose privacy, peace and quiet, and some of your basic comforts. For smaller projects, those areas under construction can be partitioned off using plastic sheeting to keep dust and mess out of your living space. But if your project includes opening an outside wall, you'll need to establish some sort of lockout system to protect your family and the rest of your home. If you experience a theft while your home is in this state, your regular home insurance may not cover it.

Moving and Storage

While the effort is Herculean, there is often no choice in a large remodel but to completely move out, store your belongings, and live elsewhere during the project. It will be yet another huge task that you'll have to orchestrate and manage. There are advantages, however:

■ Your furnishings and family treasures will remain protected in storage.

■ Workers will not disrupt your privacy or your personal space.

■ You'll have a safe, quiet refuge from the monumental mess, confusion, and frustration caused by your remodel.

There are many options for living arrangements, some more affordable than others. Important considerations include

■ Distance you'll need to travel to and from the job site.
■ The cost of maintaining two homes.
■ Impact on your family's well-being.
■ The amount of time you'll be displaced.

If you plan to return to your home while construction is still underway, ask your local building department about occupancy requirements before you move back in.

Moving to temporary living quarters during your project is yet another task you'll need to orchestrate. However, the beauty of your newly-remodeled home will make it all seem worthwhile.

Contracts

A written contract establishes your terms, conditions, and expectations for the project. Many homeowners don't bother to take this extra step and simply approve the subcontractor's bid before the work begins. While this may be fine for a small repair project, it's not a good approach for the HGC who is managing multiple subcontractors. That's because your acceptance of the bid means you tacitly approve all of your subcontractor's terms—and none of yours.

The process for developing a contract is simple:

- Carefully review your subcontractor's bid to make sure you understand the terms and the work involved.

- Inform the subcontractor that you will be drafting a contract containing the approved bid information, along with your terms and expectations.

- Draft this document, and then meet with your subcontractor to review it.

- Plan on a few rounds of revisions and reviews before both of you are happy with the contract.

- Both parties sign the contract, and each keeps a signed copy.

Don't forget to check the driver's license of your subcontractor before signing the contract. It will provide assurance that you're doing business with the person you think you're doing business with.

Be sure to include a few extra days in your schedule to allow for unexpected weather, left.

Specify fixture finishes, colors, and brands in your contracts, opposite.

Details Count. The more specific your contracts are, the better. Include material types, grade, color, model, size, weight, and thickness. Include finishes and fixtures as well. In some cases, you might also want to specify a particular brand.

Company Contracts. Some subcontractors may not be willing to sign an owner-provided contract. Instead, they may ask you to sign their company-provided contract. If this happens, you can still add your terms and conditions, project time lines, and request alternative payment plans. Regardless of whose document you use, make sure you have a signed, dated contract for the work.

Flat-Fee versus Hourly Contracts

The benefit of a flat-fee contract is that you have a fixed-cost agreement that will only change if the circumstances of the project change. Also, the subcontractor is motivated to complete the job quickly in order to move on to the next paid project. But the downside of this incentive for speed can be shoddy workmanship if you're not atten-

tive. Most professionals can accurately gauge the effort and time it will take to complete a specific project. While there may be some "padding" of hours, it's more likely that you'll get your work done on time and with more control over the project.

By the Hour. An hourly contract opens the door to other sorts of issues. The work can slow down, and it is difficult to motivate your contractor to complete on schedule. As I've said before, I do not like hourly contracts for large-scale efforts. But they can be a satisfactory option for a small job, and they may be the only way a desired subcontractor will agree to work on your project. Sometimes you just need to be flexible.

There will be times during construction when you will have to rely on the expertise and experience of your contractor to guide you. In a flat-fee contract with a set time line, you're less likely to go down a rabbit hole and get lost.

CREATING A BINDING CONTRACT

THE FOLLOWING GENERAL TERMS AND CONDI-TIONS should be included in all of your subcontractor contracts. For an example of a contract I used, see page 180.

1. Contractor will install all products per manufacturer installation procedures and recommendations. Contractor will be liable for any void of product warranty for improper installation.
2. Contractor will provide written notice for any requested changes or substitutions and will not make the change until homeowner provides written consent. Homeowner will be given one week to select replacement.
3. Contractor will provide daily cleanup of work site, including debris removal; or debris will be stored in an approved dumpster and emptied regularly. Final cleanup to be accomplished prior to final inspection.
4. This contract includes a draw schedule for payments. Draw schedule will be based on the completion of work per the project schedule.
5. Contractor agrees to provide partial release of lien as work progresses and full release of lien upon completion and final payment. Contractor will ensure that homeowner is released from all liens associated with this project and will provide a notarized final release of lien upon completion of work and receipt of final payment.
6. Existing fixtures prior to construction will remain the property of the homeowner.
7. Demolition will accommodate careful removal of specific existing fixtures, so that they are not damaged and can be reinstalled as part of the project.
8. Contractor agrees to on-time daily attendance at work site four days per week minimum, no alcoholic beverages consumed on site.
9. Contractor must provide performance and payment bond.
10. Contractor's liability policy will allow homeowner, and their agents, access for inspection of work at all times.
11. Contractor will secure job site at the end of each day and secure all supplies/tools to prevent vandalism.

12. All materials will be new, unless otherwise agreed to in writing.

13. All tool and equipment rentals, temporary services, transportation, and trash removal are the responsibility of the contractor and should be included in their bid, unless approved otherwise per this contract.

14. All permit inspections will include homeowner. Homeowner will be notified of inspection dates/time in advance.

15. Supplies will be delivered on an as-needed-only basis. Contractor will secure unused materials nightly in predetermined storage area or container to prevent theft or damage.

16. Final inspection and satisfactory completion of all items on the punch list are required before final payment.

17. Homeowner has the right to make changes to the project as needed, via a change-order process. Additional negotiated costs may incur for changes.

18. Contractor will provide homeowner with a list of suppliers who will be supplying materials to this contract (name, address, phone) and who will be providing lien releases for this project.

19. Contractor will provide homeowner with original receipts for all purchased supplies for this project.

20. All work will meet quality workmanship standards and building code requirements. Homeowner has right to cancel this contract for poor workmanship or inability or failure to meet contract requirements or terms.

21. Contractor will provide homeowner with notice of, and the right to preapprove, all unforeseen work prior to it being accomplished. Homeowner also has the right to bid out unforeseen work in the event contractor's bid is unacceptable to homeowner.

22. Contractor will provide homeowner with original receipts of building permits on building department letterhead or invoice.

23. Amenities: Homeowner is not responsible for supplying water, ice, rental equipment, telephone services, or other amenities for the contractor, his employees, or subcontractors, unless otherwise specified.

24. Owner-supplied items: See list of items owner will purchase and deliver for installation.

25. Owner-performed labor: See list of things owner will personally perform.

26. Contractor will carry a general liability insurance policy in the amount of $500,000 to $1,000,000 and will provide proof of coverage. Contractor agrees to maintain all applicable insurance policies for the duration of this project. In the event existing insurance policies expire during the construction period, contractor will provide renewal certificates as of the day of the previous policy cancellation before further payments will be made.

27. Contractor will add owner as additional insured on their company liability policy for the duration of this project.

28. An arbitration clause, stating who will arbitrate in case of a contract dispute.

Penalty Clauses

I don't believe in imposing a penalty for schedule delays. There are lots of surprises in construction—weather being one of the biggest. Appearing unreasonable won't get you very far with your workers.

If you do decide to incorporate a penalty clause in your contracts, be prepared to defend your decision, and possibly replace a contractor or two along the way. In fairness, if you include penalty clauses, you should also include reward clauses for early completion of the job.

Lien Releases

A lien release confirms that you have paid your subcontractors in full, and that they have no entitlement to place a lien on your property for unpaid construction services or materials. After the work has been completed, you will want to get a lien release from every subcontractor and materials supplier who has been involved with your project.

Don't be surprised if you get a lien notice or two from a hardware, lumber, or plumbing supplier who is providing materials to one of your subcontractors while work is underway. If this happens, make sure that your subcontractor provides you with paid receipts for all of the materials bought through these vendors. If you are making installment payments to your subcontractors, paid receipts should be provided to you at the time your payment is made.

Let your subcontractors know that you count on them and trust them, but tell them that you plan to be on job site every day to check the progress of the work.

There are a multitude of decisions to be made regarding the style and function of your new cabinetry, opposite.

Learning Curve

Contracts and Trust

While you strive to get everything right in your contracts, things don't always go exactly as planned. In my case, one subcontractor refused to sign my contract. Instead, I had to sign his standard company form, which I finally did after he let me add some of my terms to the document—not all my terms, by the way.

Another used a black pen to mark out so much of the first draft of my contract that it looked like a classified government document. We negotiated line by line on each issue he didn't like. And I had to bend a little. For yet another subcontractor—who I had known for several years—I relied upon a verbal contract.

Trust is at the heart of all of these exchanges. From the subcontractor's perspective, your terms and conditions—especially the obvious ones, such as not drinking on the job—might make him feel that you are questioning his professionalism. How you handle these interactions is crucial. Hopefully, you will use a calm and fair-minded approach because your skills in this area will speak volumes about your ability to handle other problems down the line. Protect yourself, but don't be too inflexible—and don't be surprised if the first draft of your contract provokes a little heat.

Obtaining Permits

Rules and regulations for building or remodeling a single-family home differ from one municipality to the next. Our discussion will focus on the most common permitting issues.

As the HGC, it's a great idea to visit your local building office to familiarize yourself with local ordinances. Do this even if you're working with a professional architect. For work that must meet local codes, you or your subcontractor will need to purchase a permit, and then have the local building department inspect and approve the work once it's complete.

Most municipalities have regulations for

- Building
- Drainage
- Landscaping
- Zoning
- Electrical
- Plumbing
- Mechanical
- Utility connections

Your locality may also enforce less-common regulations, such as

- Environmental protection, including trees.
- Unusual drainage issues.
- Critical area requirements, such as a steep slope or a registered historic site.

Inside Work. The building department oversees construction done inside the house. Sometimes homeowners can purchase the permit and do the work themselves. Other times the permit can only be acquired by a licensed, bonded subcontractor. In this case, your subcontractor will have to purchase the permit on your behalf and should include the fee for the permit in his bid.

You will also require a permit if you are disturbing anything outside the boundaries of your own property. This includes work that cuts into a public right of way, such as a street, sidewalk, or alley. You might have to work with your local jurisdiction to schedule this work within a specified time frame. You'll also need a permit if there will be exterior extensions of your utilities, such as water, gas, or sewer lines.

Permits and Inspections. Each type of permit also requires its own review and inspection process. Some permits will require a formal plan for building department review and feedback before work begins; other permits may only require a field inspection after the work is complete. In the latter case, you purchase the permit, do the work, and then contact your local inspector for review and approval.

Fees for permits can quickly add up, especially in a large remodel project, so be sure to budget for them.

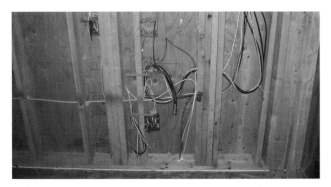

Where ordinances or codes must be met, you or your subcontractor must obtain a permit in order to perform the work, above and right.

Skipping Permits

Can you simply ignore the permitting process? The consequences for doing so can be severe. If your local building department finds out, they can require you to tear out and re-do your unlicensed work. Who will tell them you ask? A disgruntled neighbor, a subcontractor that didn't like the payment they received—just about anyone.

And don't assume that work done on the interior of your home doesn't require a permit. Let's say you decide to convert your garage into an extra bedroom. If your city has an ordinance that prohibits residents from parking on the street overnight, you're in trouble from the minute your work begins. If you ignore the process, you will be breaking the law and you won't have a place to park. So save yourself a potential headache and purchase a permit for your work if it's required.

When it's finally time to put your house on the market, your permits will prove the integrity of your home's upgrades.

The Master Building Permit

The *master building permit,* also called a *development permit,* provides you with permission to build or remodel your home according to the plan that you've provided.

Building departments use these plans and drawings to help them evaluate changes to a building.

Once you've acquired your master building permit, you can obtain all the other trade permits, such as those required for plumbing, mechanical, or sewer. These can typically be purchased without submitting further plans. The cost of a trade permit is based on the number of fixtures and features (hose bibs, faucets, toilets, etc.) you will be adding to your home.

Trade Permits

As mentioned earlier, trade permits fall under your master building permit. If there will be considerable modification to your home, you will need a master building

Check with your local building department to see what type of in-home work requires a permit in your area.

THE MASTER BUILDING PERMIT PROCESS

1. Talk with a permit specialist at your local building department to understand what local codes and ordinances will affect your project, what your building limitations are, and what your permit fees will likely be. There is typically no charge for consultation with a permit specialist at any time during the preparation of your building permit application.

2. Develop your drawings (with or without an architect) with those limitations in mind. If your remodel involves structural changes, your plans must also include engineering and design for structural support.

3. Submit your plans to the building department. This is when you (or your architect) will purchase your building permit.

4. It generally takes between two to six weeks for a building department to review plans and make

corrections to the design or engineering. Your plans will internally travel to all applicable building, zoning, and land-use departments for review and input. Rarely do plans pass through this review process without some modifications. However, most of these "corrections" are just requests for more information. The building department will then return your plans with notes on what needs correction and where you do not meet code or other requirements.

5. Using this feedback, you or your architect will correct your plans and resubmit them to the building department. Typically, plans will only go through a single correction cycle. In some cases, there can be two or three rounds of correction.

6. Once all departments have reviewed and signed off on your corrected plans, your master building permit will be issued.

Before you cover anything code-dependent, make sure that you have had it inspected, above.

Electrical permits are generally required any time electrical wiring is installed, altered, extended, or connected to any electrical equipment. Electrical permits have three inspections associated with them:

1. Rough-in inspection
2. Possible interim inspection
3. Final inspection

Plumbing permits have two or three inspections associated with them:

1. Rough-in inspection
2. Gas piping inspection
3. Final inspection

Licensed, professional contractors typically purchase mechanical permits. These include permits for furnaces, gas-line installations, and air-conditioning systems.

permit along with trade permits. If your project is less involved, you might only need one or two trade permits. Again, check with your building department to know for sure what's required in your area.

Trade permits are often inspected in phases. In the rough-in phase, piping or electrical conduit or lines are added either outside or within the house but are not yet connected to anything. Based on the complexity of the project, there may be an interim inspection or even additional permits required as part of your work. In the final inspection phase, all fixtures are in place and work is reviewed and then signed off by the local building department.

Where you can, have your subcontractors purchase necessary permits and include the cost in their bid.

The insulation inspection ensures that your insulation and ventilation systems meet applicable local energy codes.

■ Foundation Set-Back Inspection

At this inspection, the inspector will review the placement of your foundation forms by checking the plot plan and set backs, measuring where stakes are set, and ensuring that the foundation form is reinforced with steel rods. Once this inspection is passed, you can pour your new foundation footings. After they are poured, you can then begin other work, such as

1. Adding new sewer or drainage lines to your existing side sewer.
2. Installing electrical, heating, and air-conditioning conduits.

There are individual trade permits for this work, so you will need to pass those inspections before you cover any of your work. In this instance, "cover" means pouring a concrete slab over any of your new plumbing or electrical conduits, or burying your modified sewer or drainage lines.

■ Sewer Inspection

Assume that all sewer work and the connection to the city sewer line must be inspected and passed prior to being buried. Inquire about a similar inspection for septic systems.

■ Framing Inspection

The framing inspector will evaluate the structure to make sure that it is structurally sound. This means that all required sheer walls, tie downs, and joists are installed per plan; that quality materials have been used; and that the infrastructure installation (for plumbing, electrical, and HVAC) has not compromised the building's integrity. Note that the roof must be on the building at the time of the framing inspection.

Insulation Inspection

This inspection ensures that the type, thickness, and installation of your insulation and ventilation systems meet applicable local energy codes.

Drywall Nailing Inspection

Many jurisdictions require inspection of the drywall nailing to ensure it meets local codes.

Final Inspection

Your inspector will ascertain that work is complete per your plan and per code, and that all of your associated trade permits for installation of plumbing, electrical, and HVAC are complete and passed. Your final inspection provides you with permission to occupy the home and ensures that safety codes for such things as installation of guardrails, smoke detectors, windows, stairways, and doors have been met.

Building Inspections

The last piece of business before you break ground is the preconstruction inspection meeting. While not always necessary, inviting your building department inspector and your subcontractors to meet on site is a great way to ensure that you, the HGC, have everything you need to perform the work properly and pass inspections. Typically, building departments will require this type of meeting only when another expert, such as a geo-tech engineering firm, is responsible for a particular installation that the building department does not oversee.

Passing an inspection means you've obtained the building department's stamp of approval on the work you've completed. It also provides you with permission to continue building, something the industry refers to as "okay to cover." This means that you can cover up whatever was inspected and passed. Try to be on site for all building department inspections so you know what has and hasn't been completed properly.

Before you cover anything, make sure that you have had it inspected. If you don't know whether or not it needs to be inspected, call your building department.

The final inspection includes items such as the installation of handrails and the proper rise and run of stairs.

Ordering Materials

The entire goal of managing your own remodel is to save money, obtain materials that are better than those offered through a construction firm, and end up with a home that reflects more of your own tastes and preferences. The key to saving the most money is figuring out what your remodel will involve up front. This includes knowing

- Who and what will be involved.
- How much everything will cost.
- Exactly what materials you will need.
- How much time it will take to get those materials.

Gauging Lead Times. This last point is one that is often overlooked by the inexperienced homeowner. In fact, it's not unusual for a residential project to stall because someone didn't plan for lead times on the delivery of key materials, supplies, or appliances. Avoid wasting time and money by asking your suppliers early in the planning phase about their expected delivery time frame. As you collect this information, you will want to document it on your master schedule. This will prompt you to order materials in a timely manner so that they are on-site when they're needed.

Failure to preorder will not only put you behind schedule on your project, but you will also risk losing subcontractors because of the delay. Your subs are trying to manage their time in a way that earns them the most money. Most will have other projects scheduled before and after yours. It's your responsibility to have all owner-provided materials available for them when they show up to work.

Certain items have lead times as long as three to six months. Imagine the havoc it would wreak if all the windows for your second-story addition arrived three months late! While almost anything could potentially be delayed, there are some things that can be avoided.

Lumber Packages

If you're managing a remodel of any significance, it makes sense to start working on your lumber needs well before you start the project. Give yourself two to three months to finalize everything you'll need. You'll want to

work with a professional lumber company. That way, you'll be dealing with people who have experience in the home remodeling business. Go to a place that stocks everything you will need. Most lumber yards keep their lumber outdoors, which means that it is acclimated to the local humidity conditions. However, once installed, the lumber will shrink as it dries.

Visit local lumber dealers to discuss their standard lumber package and your needs, above.

In addition to kitchen and bath cabinetry, decide where you'd like other built-in cabinets, opposite.

TYPICAL LUMBER PACKAGE

YOUR LUMBER PACKAGE may include material for the following purposes

- New construction
- Nonstructural design elements, such as barge boards, enclosed soffits, fascia boards, and trim boards.
- Temporary supports (for demolition)
- Back framing lumber for:
  - Chases
  - Dropped ceilings
  - Blocking for fixtures such as towel bars, can lights, etc.

There are also customer service benefits, such as free delivery, which come with the use of a full-service lumber company. If your project is large and will require multiple deliveries and possibly add-on purchases to your lumber package, consider setting up a billing account.

Whenever you have a significant amount of material to purchase, go to the source in order to save money.

You have to be selective, too. Visit local lumber dealers to inspect their stock and find out what their standard lumber package looks like. Some lumber companies, based on who mills their lumber, will have better quality material.

While many details about your materials will be specified on your architectural plans, there are a multitude of lumber decisions that you will need to make at the lumberyard. Also, when demolition is involved, additional wood will be needed to support your home while construction is underway. In addition to materials for new construction, your lumber package may include wood

JUDGING LUMBER QUALITY

IT HELPS TO KNOW how lumber quality is determined. Interior lumber is sold in different grades based on imperfections, which include things like knots, warp, and wane. A standard package from a quality lumber company will include a selection of wood that is marked grade 1, 2, or select—all of which are appropriate for structural residential building. Grade 3 lumber is the lowest grade quality and typically only used for utility purposes or—sad to say—occasionally in spec homes. It should not be used for interior building. While there will be some imperfections in every standard package, some lumber companies offer better-quality packages overall.

Visually inspect the dimension lumber. Typically 2x6s, 2x8s, and 2x10s will have more "crown" than 2x4s. (Crown is the natural arch that you'll see when you look down the edge of a board.) The natural grain and the way that the individual piece of wood has dried affect the crown.

You may also be purchasing exterior lumber for siding, the barge board (the wood that follows the profile of your roof truss), or the fascia (the board that follows the tail of your trusses along the overhang).

Material for barge and fascia boards can, based on your budget, be comprised of

- **Cedar (either clear cedar or tight knot cedar).**
- **Primed spruce or pine.**
- **Molded plastics.**

You'll also have to make decisions on the type of sheathing you want for your roof, floor, and walls. Typical choices include plywood or oriented-strand board (OSB).

for temporary supports needed during demolition, non-structural design elements, such as fascia and barge boards, and back framing materials for dropped ceilings and fixtures. A knowledgeable supplier will ask questions about the quality and grain of lumber you'd like for particular uses.

The Take-Off. Your goal is to find a lumber supplier that is knowledgeable, professional, helpful, and eager for your business. After you've selected your lumber company based on its inventory, give them a copy of your construction plans and ask them for an estimate, or "take-off" for your project. A take-off will list all of the lumber you will need for the project by type and size. Bear in mind, however, that lumber is like gas. It's a commodity with a price that fluctuates daily. So while your take-off will give you an idea of cost, the exact amount is based on the cost of lumber on the day of purchase.

Both lumber and truss companies will complete your take-off at no charge as an incentive for you to buy your materials from them. If there is more than one lumber company offering the quality of materials and service you're seeking, you can request a take-off from each to compare prices. Because take-off calculations and formulas are not an exact science, expect some amount of shortages and overages in your lumber delivery. Also know that lumber companies don't like returns—so you may have to absorb some extra costs if you have overages. These should be no more than 10 to 15 percent of the cost of your lumber.

Time line note: Most lumber or truss companies need 10 working days to compile a take-off. For lumber purchases, expect 5 working days to get your lumber together for delivery.

Schedule a Meeting. If you're making a large purchase, ask a lumber company representative to visit your site in order to meet your framer and discuss the framing approach. This will also ensure that all lumber materials match your home and create a smooth transition with the new addition. Things to pay attention to during this visit include

- Exterior trims.
- Length of studs.
- Heights and types of materials.
- Depth of the floor system, as compared with what your plan specifies.

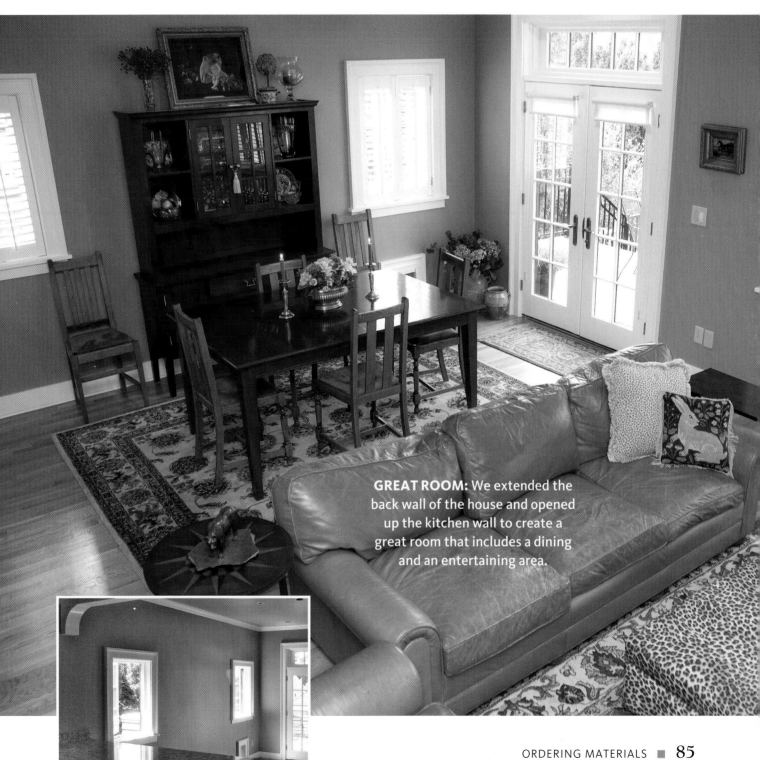

GREAT ROOM: We extended the back wall of the house and opened up the kitchen wall to create a great room that includes a dining and an entertaining area.

Trusses

Older homes typically have stick-frame roofs, which were built by hand. Today's homes often consist of factory-made trusses, which are ordered in advance, engineered to specification, and manufactured by a truss company. If your remodel includes changes to your roof, you'll want to contact a truss company to manufacture trusses to match the existing roofline.

Stick framing is labor intensive and expensive, so incorporate manufactured trusses where possible to save money.

Full Service. Some lumber companies also manufacture their own roof trusses and engineered floor joists. If you need trusses and joists along with your lumber, save money by using a company that can supply you with all of your lumber, trusses, and manufactured floor joists. There are more advantages to this than just cost.

Trusses are engineered to match the pitch and span of your roof, and to handle the natural forces of wind, snow loads, and the weight of the roofing materials. Point loads—those places where the girders of the truss will rest on top of a wall—are designed to direct the weight of what is above down through the walls of your home to the foundation.

When you have one company evaluating all these details and calculations simultaneously, you're less likely to

miss critical elements that affect the structural integrity of your home. You're also less likely to end up with the wrong lumber in the wrong place to support the planned point loads.

For Floors. Of all the lumber you purchase, the wood you buy for strong floors that won't squeak is one of your wisest investments. Avoid squeaky floors by installing I-joists.

The least expensive approach to floor joists is to use dimensional lumber, such as 2x10s or 2x12s. While this will save you money up front, there can be issues with wood shrinkage and crowning that, over time, create size differences in the joists and uneven floors. The end result is often a "squeak" in your floor. Instead, you can use pre-engineered I-joists, which come in various sizes and performance ratings. The drawback to I-joists is that the webbing cannot be cut to allow mechanical systems to pass through as would happen with a typical solid two-by floor joist.

If you have ducts or other mechanical systems that will pass through an area of your home that requires floor joists, consider having your truss company manufacture floor trusses. Built from 2x4s with an open web design, a custom floor truss can accommodate mechanical systems, such as piping and ducts, while still providing the benefits of a factory-made system.

Manufactured roof trusses, opposite, and I-joists, below, are good alternatives to stick-framing on-site. Both help ensure quality results.

Furnaces, Gas Fireplaces, and Hot-Water Heaters

Like kitchen appliances, each of these units may have to be ordered directly from a manufacturer and have a lead time associated with delivery. Know the order time line and work with your supplier to deliver your systems around the time they will be needed at the site by your subcontractor.

Plumbing Fixtures

Where you end up purchasing your plumbing fixtures will make a difference either in the upfront cost or the risk for replacement. Access to wholesale plumbing supply houses—outlets where professionals can purchase high-quality plumbing fixtures at reasonable costs—remain off-limits for most homeowners. If your plumber is willing, you might be able to convince him to allow you to purchase your fixtures, at cost, under his contractor's business account, through his wholesale supplier. This is a win for you because you'll get 100 percent warranty-backed fixtures along with your plumber's professional guarantee. In other words, if something fails after the work is complete, replacements and repairs are at no cost to you. You'll also have access to a highly knowledgeable plumbing fixture expert who can purchase whatever you want through a network of valuable resources, saving you both worry and time.

If you do not use a wholesale supplier, make sure that you work with someone who can help you understand all the fixture parts and pieces your plumber will need and

ensure that your purchases work together in both function and design.

Appliances

For resale value, the look of your kitchen appliances is as important as their features and performance. While you can easily purchase appliances from multiple manufacturers and retailers, you'll need to match colors and styles from different sources. If your cooktop is stainless steel with black knobs and accents, do not purchase a white dishwasher to save a few bucks.

If you order a gas fireplace directly from the manufacturer, above, be sure to build some lead time for delivery into your schedule.

Find out whether your plumber is willing to let you purchase your fixtures, below, for cost under his business account.

PURCHASING APPLIANCES

HERE ARE SOME TIPS that will be helpful as you work out a solution to your own appliance situation:

- Shop at stores that specialize in appliances only, as they're more flexible in their ability to modify delivery options and installation times to suit your needs.
- Shop at stores with a wide variety of manufacturers and a large inventory, and plan to purchase all of your appliances from a single store. This gives you more clout when you make special requests.
- Negotiate with your retailer before the sale to determine whether they're willing to hold off on delivery of your purchased appliances until your remodel is finished.

If you're replacing all of your kitchen appliances, there will likely be a tipping point in the shopping process. You'll find a fridge, stove, or dishwasher that will be too hard to pass up. From that point on, the savings you're able to realize on the purchase of your remaining appliances is secondary to their ability to "fit in" with the appliance style you've already chosen.

When to Buy. Even though your appliances are the last items to add to your home after a remodel, you're more likely to save money if you take advantage of appliances sales, which may mean purchasing them before or during construction. The trick for the HGC is figuring out where to store the appliances during the project. Keeping them in a construction area is a recipe for damage. While you can easily get delivery and installation from the retailer, if you end up storing appliances for a long period of time, you may be faced with a second appliance move and the need to pay for installation.

Save money by taking advantage of appliance sales rather than delaying your purchase until you're ready to install them.

Doors and Windows

There are a number of things to consider when it comes to the purchase of doors and windows, such as whether or not you want to match your existing units, whether you want them primed or painted at the factory, and who will install them. Because doors and windows are manufactured in specific sizes, purchasing standard-sizes will save you significant money.

If you are replacing older, existing doors and windows that are not standard sizes, it may be cheaper to replace the original units with standard-size products and pay for the additional framing rather than order custom doors or windows. But if replicating a certain "look" is important, additional framing cannot accommodate the job, or these changes create other construction issues, then custom units may be your only option.

There are all kinds of problems that can occur with windows at the time of construction and later. Choose a supplier who is willing and able to help you if things go wrong.

If you plan to purchase multiple doors and windows, save yourself money and deal with the larger door and window manufacturers. And for heaven's sake—visit the showrooms. Have someone walk you through each type of unit so that you understand your options. Not only will you gain the information you need to make the right choice, but you'll also understand how the manufacturer handles problems and backs their products.

Selecting Doors. Buying the doors for your project is one of the most exciting purchases you'll make. Your choice should reflect your taste and the style of your new home. Your door package will include interior and exterior doors, as well as closet doors. While a good door manufacturer will provide great assistance in developing a comprehensive door package, it's up to you to make sure that you choose the right door for each door opening and to provide exact measurements (once the drywall phase is complete) so that all of your doors are manufactured correctly. One of the worst scenarios is to tear out drywall and studs to install a door that is too large for the opening.

It was news to me that doors typically come prehung. This means that you get not only the door but also the frame. If you're thinking about refurbishing older doors to be reused in your remodel, understand that there is a lot of extra work and cost to that effort. First, it's often difficult to remove an older doorframe intact, which means that while you can salvage the door, you

probably can't reuse the frame. If your old doors need to be professionally refinished, expect to pay an additional $100–$800 per door. That alone is easily the cost of a new, prehung door. Then there is the hardware issue. Older hardware is costly to install on new doors because today's doors have hole sizes for modern hardware. If you do install older hardware, plan on constant maintenance to keep it working properly.

Ordering Time Line. You'll work up a comprehensive door order, select all the hardware in advance, and then wait until your framing contractor is finished with the framing *before* you order the doors. You do this so that each door exactly matches the framed opening of the doorways and closets. Here are a few things to think about when ordering doors from a manufacturer:

1. Know what doorknobs and locking hardware you plan to install because the manufacturer will predrill holes in your door to fit that hardware. This means you have to finalize your choice before you buy the doors. You can, however, order the hardware later in the build phase.

2. Know what style and type of door hinges you want for the same reasons.

3. Be clear on which way the door should swing so that hardware holes are properly placed on your door. This requires a close look at your plans. You don't want doors opening in a manner that will block access to something. Have the door swing toward a blank wall whenever possible.

4. Don't forget about closet doors, utility-room doors, and exterior doors. These may have different knobs or locking systems.

It may be cheaper to replace original windows with standard-size new windows, opposite. Also, standardize trim styles throughout your home. We even copied the trim used around windows on our doggie doors, left.

WINDOWS AND ENERGY SAVINGS

YOU'LL FIND THAT WINDOWS ARE RATED according to their performance in certain areas. Here is a quick overview of window glazing performance standards to help you compare different manufacturers and options:

- U-values measure the window's resistance to heat loss. The lower the U-factor, the better the insulation performance.
- Solar heat gain coefficient tells how well the window blocks heat from the sun. The lower the number, the more heat it blocks.
- VLT stands for visible light transmittance. VLT measures the percent of light the glazing on your window lets in as compared to a ⅛-inch-thick sheet of clear glass. This is associated with the window's ultraviolet value. This value lists the extent that the glazing will prevent fading of fabrics in the home.
- There is also the Energy Star seal, which means the window meets minimum energy requirements.

Buying Windows. While glazing performance, basic window type, and hinging may be listed on your architectural drawings, there are a wide variety of other features to choose from. Things to consider are

- Window type: casement, awning, double-hung, slide, non-operational.
- Window frame type: vinyl, wood, aluminum, fiberglass, composite.
- Color.
- Screens.
- Hardware, including locks, cranks, and handles.
- Operation and type of opening.
- Grills or muntins.
- Hinging (which way the window swings to open).

The fact that there are so many choices should alert you to the need to get out there, and get busy on your window selection. But even more important is the need to choose windows that fit the rough openings for windows indicated on your plans, and to order them well enough in advance that you will receive the order when your window installer is on-site and ready to do his work.

Window Companies. Some manufacturers can provide you with doors, windows, and skylights as well. Others will specialize only in windows, or doors, or skylights, which will require you to purchase individual items separately through several companies. Regardless of whom you use, window and door manufacturers typically provide a take-off at no charge using your blueprints. Your architect may already have developed a generic window or door schedule as part of your drawings. This will provide you with a basic idea of what you need and serve as a starting point for you in your discussions with manufacturers and retailers. But there is still a lot of work to do before you actually purchase your windows and doors. Once you've chosen a particular manufacturer, you'll develop a much more detailed window or door schedule with information such as

- Window and door opening measurements.
- A graphic, showing the type of window and operation.
- Screen information.
- Hardware.
- Glazing.
- Color (Primed).

Compare your detailed window or door schedule from your supplier with the floor plan view of your construction drawings to ensure that all of your windows and doors are included.

Do not compare your list with the elevation views of your drawings. These views provide an idea of the finished look of the home and are not as accurate as the floor-plan views when it comes to developing a detailed schedule. Go over your schedule with your window representative several times to make sure that you've caught everything. In my own remodel, it took us at least three reviews before we were both sure that all 27 windows and accessories were correct.

GREAT ROOM: Having rooms filled with natural light was very important to us. Our architect specified a variety of window and door options.

Get It in Writing. Ultimately, your contract with a door or window supplier should include all the details about the product, as well as a clear statement about who is doing the installation. When a manufacturer or window supplier offers window installation, be sure you know what that means—and take a minute to evaluate if it is a good choice for you. For the homeowner involved in a whole-house remodel, manufacturer-provided installation might be more than you need, especially if you already have a framer or some other construction expert available to set the windows properly, and you can manage trim and paint through your other subcontractors at a cheaper price.

After you've finalized your schedules and confirmed installation, you should receive a line-item contract from

Windows are part of "dry in" phase of construction where a completely enclosed space is achieved. That's why it's critical that you coordinate your window ordering with your framing contractor.

your supplier. It's standard to pay 100 percent of your window and door costs up front. You'll then set the order date for your windows and doors based on your construction schedule. It's common practice to place the window order on the day the lumber drops. Assume two to three months from the time you order your windows and doors until the time they will be delivered. Of course,

EXTERIOR DOORS USED ON THIS PROJECT

BASEMENT APARTMENT

GARAGE

many things can impact your manufacturing time line, including the time of year (summer has the longest lead time), so keep in touch with your window supplier to confirm delivery requirements and availability.

Be Prepared. With a large remodel, your window and door purchase will be a substantial investment. Don't let sticker shock overwhelm you. Windows and doors are highly visible, important features of your home. Make the right choice, and you'll increase the value of your home through heating and cooling performance and curb appeal. Choose a quality manufacturer, buy direct, and shop smart. If you succeed, you'll have a 20-year guarantee at full replacement value and a transferable warranty.

FRONT ENTRY

Learning Curve

"The Right Stuff"

Because I grew up during the era when feminism was in full swing, I don't have a lot of preconceived notions about what a woman can't or shouldn't do. So I was surprised to discover that in some places, gender discrimination is apparently still alive and well.

At a very busy window-supply store I visited, the place was filled with men—general contractors, workers, and an all-male sales staff. Naturally, I waited patiently for my turn. Fifteen minutes turned into 30, then 45. An hour passed before someone finally approached me to ask, "Do you need something?"

After a lengthy question-and-answer session during which I sensed my painful ignorance, I decided on a particular window and door manufacturer and gave the salesperson my plans so that he could create a bid for me. He asked if he could have two weeks to pull together the figures. No problem.

Two weeks later, I called to review his proposal. He was out of town. Three weeks later, he was on the golf course. On the fourth week, I showed up at the store, asked for my plans back, and left. No one gave me a follow-up call. Why? Perhaps because I was woman, and it was obvious that I was not a construction professional, this store didn't consider my business to be worth pursuing.

Aside from the blow to my self-esteem—or perhaps because of it—I learned that making good purchasing decisions is not only about finding the best materials at a good price, but it is also about choosing the right people with whom to do business.

Cabinetry and Countertops

When it comes to cabinets, it's all about doing your homework ahead of time. You'll want to provide your subcontractors with the exact sizes and locations of your cabinets and appliances so that they can frame the room properly and bring plumbing and gas service to the right locations.

Today there is a world of choice when it comes to where and how to purchase and install cabinetry. For built-ins, you can use a custom-cabinet maker, order from a retail store, hire an on-site finish carpenter, or save money by using prefabricated cabinet frames from a discount store and upgraded doors from a higher-end supplier. You can also purchase freestanding cabinets or, in the case of a bathroom, create your own cabinets by converting a piece of existing furniture. Unless you're purchasing prefabricated cabinets off the floor of a retail store, there is likely a lead-time for delivery.

> Like windows, there are a multitude of decisions to be made with cabinets— the look, their ease of use, storage space, and the impact on traffic flow.

The Custom Route. Custom-cabinetry manufacturers will typically come to your home to discuss your needs, take measurements, and provide you with a schematic layout/design. They can also deliver and install your cabinets after they've arrived. Cabinet dealers and many retailers offer design services as well. You provide the measurements and they work up a cabinet layout using semicustom or standard cabinets.

In addition to kitchen and bath cabinetry, now is the time to think about where other built-in cabinets will be included in your home, and who will build, install, and finish them.

Countertops. Once you have finalized what material to use for your countertops, you'll be able to determine the work associated with their installation. Some materials, such as laminate, can be purchased close to the time

KITCHEN: We wanted to open the kitchen to the new great room and create a seating bar with a granite countertop.

of installation while others, such as granite, will require advanced ordering, storage of materials, and the use of a fabricator or other trade specialist.

Countertops can be comprised of multiple materials to suit multiple needs. Some top choices, and the benefits, drawbacks, and construction implications of each are discussed in Chapter 8.

The Job Site

As the HGC, you're responsible for the safety of everyone on your property during construction. This includes not only keeping the construction site orderly and clean, and clearly marking off dangerous areas, but also making sure that the work is performed according to best safety practices.

Keep the construction site orderly and clean so that people don't trip and fall over things.

A Safe Environment. If you've hired licensed professionals, they'll already have their own safety equipment and will know how to complete their job. However, if you add on work outside of a contractor's normal job description—for instance, asking your carpenter to run piping through your roof—it's your job to provide safety equipment.

Another safety concern involves how to keep people off your property during construction. Options include "No Trespassing" signs or construction fencing rented from a local fence company. These portable chain-link fences can be hauled in and set up within a few short hours by the fencing company. When the project requires heavy equipment access, be sure to include a rented gate system along with it. Purchase a chain and padlock, and lock the gate at the end of each workday. Make sure you're on-site early, or provide the key to your workers so that you don't slow things down.

Safety of the contents of the rest of your home and your family is a concern when your remodel includes removal of an exterior wall, window, or doorway. For windows or doors, use plywood that is secured inside the opening using lag bolts and 2x4s. This solution will not damage your door or window frame and provides a safe barrier to entry.

Check out your state's department of labor and industries website for safety equipment requirements.

Call your local utilities so that they can survey and flag all underground gas, water, and power lines, below left.

Use plywood secured with lag bolts and 2x4s to protect your door frame and provide a barrier to entry, below.

The Amenities. You'll also need to make arrangements for basic facilities, such as a restroom for workers and electricity to provide light and run power tools. At different points in the construction process, your workers will also need access to other amenities, such as water and heat.

If you're living in another part of your home while construction is underway, you may not want workers tromping through to use your bathroom. An easy solution that you are required to supply if you're completely gutting and rebuilding your home is to rent a portable toilet. You want the portable toilet on-site so that workers don't waste valuable time going to and from the restroom. Find a local supplier on the Internet or in the local phone directory. Typically there's a flat fee for drop off and pick up, and you'll be billed monthly after that. Service includes regular cleaning and restocking of supplies.

Cleanup. Finally, you'll need to think about trash. The building process is messy. Not only will you have discarded fixtures and demolition materials, but almost everything you install will come with packaging. Renting a dumpster is a good idea for a large project. The trick is figuring out where to place it. If you don't rent a dumpster, at the very minimum allocate an area for trash and scraps and regularly dispose of them. Be careful, however, not to throw wood scraps away too early in the construction process. You might find these useful later on. Set aside a scrap-wood pile in addition to your trash area.

> Save any lumber 2 feet in length or longer, to be used for back framing, temporary supports, and miscellaneous carpentry work.

Protecting the Environment. As part of the permitting process, your local building department may specify local land and environment protection requirements, such as erosion and sediment control. These supplies can be purchased at a home center and are easily installed.

One technique designed to reduce mud and protect topsoil during spring or fall construction is to lay down a

A portable toilet for workers is a requirement if you're completely gutting and rebuilding your home.

layer of straw over the exposed ground. You might have to renew the bed of straw as time progresses. In a residential area, this can create quite a stir. Once, right after we laid straw, a local neighbor and his young daughter walked by. I overheard the little girl ask excitedly, "Dad, do they have a pony in there?"

Another technique to prevent ruts and trenches from forming in high-traffic areas is to lay down OSB board to serve as a temporary sidewalk.

Utility Notifications. For projects that involve digging of any kind, call your local utilities well in advance and have them survey and flag all underground gas, water, cable/telephone, and power lines. If your project includes upgrades to your utilities, you'll also need to call and schedule the service shut-off.

Because electrical power is necessary at all times during construction, if your project disrupts the electrical service location or main panel of your home, your electrical contractor will need to set up temporary electrical service.

Preconstruction Meeting

Before you start demolition, excavation, or construction work on your property, gather your key players together for a powwow. Your goal is to review the blueprints and talk through each step of the construction process together as a team. This meeting accomplishes more than just reviewing previously discussed plans. It provides an opportunity for each subcontractor to hear the proposed actions of the other subcontractors. Because each depends upon the expertise of the contractor who does the work prior to them, they'll have a chance to evaluate the handoff points—where their role begins, and at what point in the process "ownership" of the project falls to them.

MEETING ATTENDEES

- Architect
- Demolition contractor
- Excavation contractor
- Foundation/footings contractor
- Framing contractor
- Roofing contractor
- Sewer/plumbing contractor
- Electrical contractor

Evaluating the Schedule. This meeting also provides the first critical look at the master schedule and construction sequence that you've planned. With their combined experience, your team of subcontractors can help you identify any gaps or missing players in the process. Your job is to lead the meeting, but let your experts talk through their work, ask each other questions, and help you develop solutions to any problems that arise. As professionals, their training is to create the most streamlined and efficient process possible to complete their portion of the work and move on. They'll also be evaluating the professionalism of each other. The ability to count on, respect, and understand the approach and overall plan of the preceding contractor will provide them with the assurance that you, as the HGC, know what you're doing, and that the project will run smoothly.

Handoff Meetings

As I've said before, your framing contractor relies on the expertise of the foundation contractor; your painting contractor relies on the expertise of the drywall contractor; and so on. Because of this interdependency, it's your job to invite the follow-on contractor to the job site prior to the time that their own work begins to ensure that everything that they'll need to begin work is being completed. You should be present at this meeting to facilitate the discussion and mediate concerns that may arise.

At handoff meetings, your job is to hear how the work is coming along, pay attention to what else needs to be done to support ongoing construction, and make sure that any obstacles are handled. Your willingness to respond to the needs of your subcontractors will speed construction and create an environment of professionalism and trust. The end result is better performance from your workers and a job well done.

Your willingness to listen to the concerns of your subcontractors helps to create a positive, professional environment, left.

Give your subcontractors the exact location of your fixtures so that they can bring plumbing to the right spot, opposite.

Demolition

Very few of us think about taking apart our home when we first consider remodeling. The reality is that the old needs to be removed before anything new can be built. Demolition is a preconstruction task as well as the first step of construction.

Depending upon the size of your project, demolition will either be easy or a monumental effort. The cost of demolition depends, like any other work effort, on the amount of labor, expertise, and materials required. This work can be complex and even dangerous. Sometimes, it can even present the opportunity to make money by recycling valuable fixtures or features that you no longer want.

Working in Stages. Demolition is not always a one-time event. In a large remodel, demolition may be done in stages so that the basic structure of the building remains sound. Dismantling your home has the potential to compromise both the short- and long-term structural integrity of your house, as well as the physical safety of your workers.

The process creates an enormous amount of trash, which needs proper disposal. And there are health concerns, such as the removal of hazardous materials, including asbestos and lead paint. Because of these concerns, it's important to select a good demolition contractor.

Most people have little or no knowledge of their local demolition resources. You'll need a fully licensed and insured subcontractor with an excellent reputation. In addition to verifying your contractor's credentials, there are a few extra requirements.

Take advantage of your demolition contractor's interest in your recyclable items by negotiating with him or her for a reduced fee or for dump-fee credits in return for your recyclable items.

Find Cash in the Trash. In some areas, recyclables such as copper, brass, and lead can be sold on the secondary market for up to $2 per pound. For the most part, recycling should be completed before demolition. Materials such as piping, wiring, or heavy, installed items can be recycled in conjunction with demolition if that is part of your contract with the demolition company. If you have a separate recycling company on board, you'll need to have the work complete before the demolition team begins.

Demolition is both a preconstruction task and the first step of construction, opposite.

In a large remodel, you may have construction interspersed with demolition so that the basic structure of your house remains sound, below.

BID WALK THROUGH

DURING YOUR WALK THROUGH with your demolition contractor

1. Point out areas that need to be safeguarded or protected from damage.
2. Make sure your contractor fully understands the scope of the work. Do this by reviewing the plans together at the site.
3. Outline a plan and time lines for the work phases.
4. Establish a location for the dumpster.
5. Take notes so that you can include all of your agreements regarding scope of work and scheduling in your contractor contract.

Getting a Demo Bid. As with other qualified contractors, bring the demolition contractor to the job site and show the company representative your working plans so that the company can provide you with the most accurate bid. Use the bid meeting to discuss details of how demolition might be accomplished, what items to save or recycle, and what will be included in the work.

During your bid walk throughs, point out items that need to be protected from damage.

DEMOLITION CONTRACT ITEMS

THE DEMOLITION CONTRACT should contain items on

- **Recyclables.** Who, what, when, where, and how much.
- **Garbage disposal.** On-site dumpster location, frequency of dump runs, dump receipts.
- **Demolition phases.** Approximate time lines for each phase of demolition and the specific plan for when and how to remove walls, roof, etc.
- **Clear instructions** on how much to demolish,

such as "demolish wall to studs" or "demolish and remove entire wall."

- **De-nailing.** Who will remove the nails from any remaining studs? This must be done prior to framing.
- **Hazardous materials.** Plan for handling removal and disposal.
- **Installation of protection** for remaining portions of the home. This includes temporary doors, padding and covering for countertops and cabinets, installation of material to protect hardwood floors, structural supports needed, and the like.

Protecting Your Home

Before your demolition begins, make sure that you've removed everything that you want to keep. This includes hardware from doors and cabinets, light fixtures and lightbulbs, all personal items, and anything to be recycled. For a large remodel this can take days, so give yourself enough time.

Working with the Demolition Team. Show up at the site on the first day of demo to make sure that the demolition team leader knows what to do. Review the scope of work briefly, especially if the lead person is not the same one who came to bid your job. If there's any disconnect between what you talk about, and what they've been told, sort it out immediately. Once work starts, the demo team will begin with the protection phase—covering vulnerable areas, such as floors and windows, before they'll begin the dismantling work. Pay attention so that nothing's missed.

Then steel yourself for the violent destruction that marks the beginning of your new, wonderfully improved home!

Protect hardwood floors and reduce the mess by having your demolition contractor lay down two layers of hardboard material on the floor. You'll remove the top layer after drywall work is complete and have a clean job site for painting and finish carpentry work.

Learning Curve

The Case for a Clean Job Site

My husband, Bart, never understood why it was so important for me to constantly tidy up the house even when it was a complete construction zone. I guess it's because when you love a place, and it's been your home, it's hard to let go of that ownership. You still care for it, as if it were a sick and disheveled family member, and treat it with dignity and respect. I cleaned constantly, and there was a lot to clean up. Old lumber scraps, sawdust, package wrappers, bent nails, and lunch-box leavings. During the day, I was careful to do my thing only in those areas where no one was working, lest I disrupt the flow. Looking back, I would say that picking up trash and moving stuff around so that I could sweep was the second biggest job I had as the HGC. Because I failed to budget for a dumpster, bags and bags of trash that should have been hauled away every week grew into a humongous pile that became a hangout for the local crows.

If I had to do it over again, I'd rent a dumpster. Instead, we spent our weekends loading a rented pickup truck with junk. Using the yard as a trash site meant we had to clean up twice. However, I think that keeping the house tidy was a good move. The workers saw my concern and, at the end of the day, they did their best to clean up, too. What's more, there was very little theft because I left my broom marks in every corner of the house.

Demolition creates an enormous amount of trash, which requires proper disposal. There may also be environmental concerns, as in the removal of hazardous materials.

CHAPTER 6

A BUILDING OVERVIEW

Day-to-Day Details

As a first-time HGC, there are many aspects of construction that you probably haven't thought much about. After all, most homeowners don't need to know exactly how to attach a new porch to their existing structure or where a particular plumbing pipe is located behind a wall. But these are precisely the kinds of details you must confront if you're planning on ripping apart and rebuilding some or most of your house.

Before I became my own general contractor, I lacked the basic knowledge of home construction I needed to understand the big picture. How would I know if things were being done in the right way? What pitfalls should I avoid because they could put my house—or my family—in danger? How could I prioritize my worries so that those wakeful hours of the night could be more productively spent on truly important concerns?

This chapter provides the answers to these questions. We will cover the basic types of work involved in a home remodel, and I will provide some perspective on where you can give yourself a little breathing room.

Landscaping

Landscaping may be the last step in completing your remodel, but it's one of the first things you need to think about when you're planning to expand your home. In particular, how will the remodel affect your existing property? If you're moving outside walls, you might have to remove some big-ticket items, such as trees, outbuildings, and existing plantings, then reinstall sidewalks, steps, driveways, and landscaping when the work is finished.

Getting the Most from Subs. Knowing exactly what needs to go will help you make the best use of your contractors. It will also save you money because you can include the work in their contracts now instead of adding it on later.

For example, if you know that you'll have to re-route a sidewalk, it makes sense to include its removal as part of your agreement with your excavator, even though your primary use of that contractor may be to dig new foundation footings and walls.

Other than removing items, don't invest in plants or be too quick to restore your yard, gardens, and hardscapes (patios, walkways, and driveways) until all of your work is complete.

Knowing what to expect helps to avoid problems. We had to plan for vents for our gas fireplace.

Outdoor Lighting

Today's outdoor lighting solutions have progressed way beyond the bug light on the porch. Good exterior lighting is a large part of your home's facade. Features to think about as you consider your remodel include

- Embedded lighting in concrete porches or steps.
- Lighting for paths, walkways, or patios.
- Garden or special-feature lighting, such as lighting for a fountain.
- Electrical outlets for holiday lights.

DON'T SKIMP ON THE FACTS

YOU WILL NEED TO PROVIDE as much information as possible so that your subcontractors will understand what you want. Creating drawings, taking measurements, and getting photographs from all angles take time and effort. Do not expect anyone else to do this for you—as the HGC, it's your job!

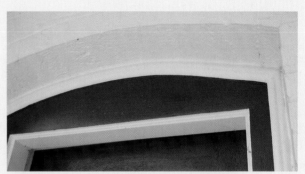

Here are just some of the photos I provided to my subcontractors so that they could use newer materials to duplicate the look of our 1925-era porch.

THE NEW ENTRY

There are unlimited configurations for your yard, so it makes sense to consider your options and embed this work in your contracts with subcontractors. A new outdoor lighting design will require excavation, conduit pipe and cable, back fill, and installation of fixtures.

Sprinklers

As with exterior lighting, installing an irrigation system is one more option that can be planned for in advance. However, installing sprinklers is a fairly simple and easy project for any homeowner and can be done well after your remodel is complete. Should you choose to include this work in your remodel project, be sure to have the system properly installed, and be aware that your local jurisdiction may inspect it regularly.

Backflow Prevention. Sprinkler systems can create a vacuum effect and draw dirt into the municipal water lines. This would contaminate the city's main water line, for which you would be heavily fined. In some areas, yearly inspections may be required by your local jurisdiction to ensure that your backflow preventer remains operational.

Exterior Fixtures and Features

The style, shape, and proportion of your exterior fixtures and features can make or break your home's design. While there are beautiful homes almost everywhere, you'll find plenty of "what not to do's" within the same neighborhoods. If you own an older home and plan to reproduce a particular feature or fixture, don't automatically assume that a simple photograph or two will provide your subcontractors with all the information they need to give you what you want. Remember, building is a creative process, and there are many ways to put things together. What's more, today's craftsmen are experienced in today's styles, not in something from the past. So it's possible that anyone you hire will need detailed measurements and drawings along with photographs to understand how you want your home to look at its completion. As mentioned earlier, you have to know exactly what you want if you expect others to understand your vision.

Structure and Infrastructure

Your structural foundation needs to be perfect. If you're extending your home, adding on a second level or room, or modifying the footprint in any way, spend money on hiring the most experienced and professional foundation and footing subcontractor you can find. A level and correct foundation helps ensure that your framing will also be successful.

Your Worst Enemy. Water holds the potential to destroy all your efforts and make a mess of your home. As you work from the ground up, protect your investment by installing footing and storm drains; then, as you frame and enclose your home, make sure that you hire an expert siding contractor. You want a tight, secure building envelope—but not so tight that your home can't "breathe." So make sure you pay attention to proper ventilation. Having a well-constructed envelope with windows and doors properly installed will result in a home that can last up to 100 years. With water intrusion problems, you could have less than six weeks.

Behind the Walls. The second most important part of construction is your infrastructure, meaning everything that goes behind the walls. A house's infrastructure includes mechanical systems such as heating, plumbing, air conditioning, and electrical. It's important to have this

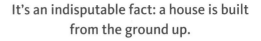

It's an indisputable fact: a house is built from the ground up.

work done properly and to have everything you'll eventually want and need installed while your walls are open. Reworking infrastructure after the fact is both messy and expensive. You'll have to remove trim, drywall, or flooring to reach it and then restore these layers later. However, if something is forgotten or a small mistake is made, you can go back and fix it. It's not as catastrophic as a poorly poured foundation where your entire house could collapse, or crooked framing, where all your walls are off-kilter.

Contractor Pecking Order. You'll be working with a plumber, heating contractor, and electrical contractor during the infrastructure phase of construction. While each one of them will ask to have first choice in where their system will be installed and how it will be routed, standard construction practice says that the plumber will choose his routing first, followed by the heating/air conditioning contractor, and then the electrical contractor. This means that the electrical contractor will work around the first two systems.

Finishes and Surfaces

This part of construction deals with such elements as drywall, flooring, and countertops. Flaws in installation or failure to use good-quality materials will greatly affect the overall look of your home. Finishes and surfaces are a main target of later remodels and of post-remodel fixes, too. Replacing carpeting with hardwood flooring, adding an art nook to a wall, or upgrading your countertops from laminate to granite are just a few later changes. The key for the HGC is having a vision of the end game. What's the ultimate goal of your remodel? Cost may preclude you from adding a granite countertop to your kitchen during

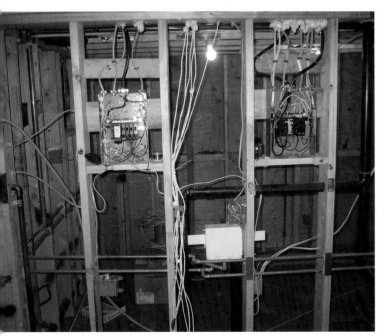

Houses work because of what is hidden within the walls and floors. Plan the routing of electrical, plumbing, and HVAC equipment carefully.

BUTLER'S PANTRY: We wanted a walk-in pantry off of the kitchen.

the initial remodel, but is this something you'll be adding later? If so, build with that plan in mind, and be sure to purchase cabinetry that will accommodate the weight of that material for later installation.

In this category of construction you'll be dealing with drywallers, painters, countertop fabricators, and flooring and tile installers.

Interior Fixtures and Features

While seemingly incidental, your interior fixtures and features are the most visible part of your remodel. They're also what give your home its unique charm and livability. Everyone who sees your home will judge your success as the general contractor by the professional look of this portion of your project. Doesn't that inspire you to spend some time reviewing the interior features and fixtures you'll want to include?

A house is filled with so many of these features that most people don't think about them—unless they're not there. Just how nice is that new closet without shelving or a door? How about doors and windows that lack trim or a kitchen without cupboards? However, if you're trying to save money or have used up your remodel budget, most fixtures—with the exception of safety items such as stair railings—can wait until you're flush again. You might be a bit inconvenienced and possibly a little shy about having guests over, but you can easily complete this phase of construction over an extended period of time. Just don't make the mistake of leaving your home incomplete forever.

Architectural Features. Architectural elements, however, are a different matter. These include coved ceilings, door archways, built-ins, and newel posts for banisters. These features are extremely expensive—if not impossible—to add after the fact. You DO need to plan for them early in construction because as part of the structure they affect framing.

THE CONSTRUCTION SEQUENCE

NEW ADDITIONS—where the outside walls of your home are expanded out—are just like new houses in that they are also built from the ground up. The sequence of demolition and the methods used for supporting the rest of your home during construction depend upon what you're removing and what rests above or adjacent to that area.

Remodeling is a dynamic process in which you're destroying something old in order to create something new. In your own remodel, the parts of your home that

EXCAVATING FOR THE FOUNDATION

FRAMING THE BASEMENT

FRAMING THE THIRD FLOOR

SHEATHING THE EXTERIOR

are removed and how work will be accomplished around what's left will probably differ from what occurred during my project. You must work with your own team of experts to come up with a sequenced plan of action. But it's important to have some idea of what it's going to take—and what is possible to achieve.

The pictures here tell the story of how my own home was taken apart and rebuilt. Because the entire floor plan was changed, these pictures illustrate the creation of new rooms throughout the whole house. The original configuration of the house bears very little resemblance to what is illustrated here. It's a magical, fairy-tale kind of story in which closets were transformed into stairwells, a cramped attic bedroom was turned into a light-filled second story, and a dungeon disappeared completely.

FRAMING THE MAIN-LEVEL ADDITION

REAR DECK

FRONT ENTRY

LIVING ROOM

WINDOW-SEAT ROOM

MASTER BEDROOM

MASTER BATHROOM

BASEMENT APARTMENT

BASEMENT BATHROOM

DINING AND FAMILY ROOM

KITCHEN

OFFICE/BEDROOM #1

OFFICE/BEDROOM #2

GARAGE

YARD AND GARDENS

Delivery and Storage of Materials

Good construction management includes getting your construction materials on-site just as they're needed. Not too early, because you don't want them taking up valuable working space, getting lost, or damaged during the construction process; and not too late, because that will slow down the work.

You need to constantly monitor where you are in the building process so you can know how soon a particular item will be needed. You do this by continually talking to your workers and then communicating to your manufacturers how the work is progressing compared to the estimated time line you provided on your master schedule.

Delivery Options. Who delivers your materials is an important issue. Unless it's specifically stated in your written agreements, you'll be doing it yourself. That means having the right vehicle and loading and unloading it. If you think this sounds like a lot of work—it is. So try to avoid it. Wherever possible, get your suppliers to deliver materials to your job site—especially if the fee is nominal. When you take into consideration your time and effort and the cost of a truck, it's a good value. When your supplier will not deliver, hire a construction helper who has a strong back, does not mind lifting, and knows how to be careful.

In addition to costly or bulk items, such as plumbing fixtures, appliances, windows and doors, and siding, there will be many days when a few extra pieces of lumber or hardware will be needed. Plan to be at the site on a daily basis to monitor materials and make sure that shortages do not hold up the work. You can save money by making quick runs to the lumber supplier yourself, or you can hire someone to be your "runner." In either case, expect it.

Let Everyone Know That You Know. Once your materials arrive, you need to inspect them, count them, and store them in a safe place. Mark the number of each item clearly, and make sure that your workers know that you know what materials are accounted for and on the site. This can be done discreetly by saying something like, "Gene's Plumbing Supply has just delivered all of the plumbing fixtures for all four bathrooms. I've inventoried and stored them along the back wall of the basement bedroom because I think they'll be out of your way there. Let me know if that's a problem for you." This habit will help keep materials from walking off the job.

Windows and Doors

You'll need a protected, indoor space to store windows and doors once they arrive from the manufacturer. They should come labeled by item number and wrapped for protection. Inspect them immediately because they can be damaged in shipping. A good manufacturer will stand behind its product and replace any damaged inventory. As you inspect your new windows and doors, write in the rough opening dimensions and the number of the window, as listed on your detailed schedule, on the factory label. By tying your windows directly to the working blueprint, you are helping your framer or installer know exactly what window or door goes in what location.

Don't expect miracles from delivery drivers. Timing is not always perfect and you may have to wait.

LIVING ROOM:
We decided on a
semi-formal entry
that leads to
the living room
through an arched
opening.

Lumber

If you've purchased a large lumber package, you can expect your lumber company to deliver it for free in two to three deliveries. If you order more lumber after that, and those orders are not full lumber packages, expect them to charge you for each additional delivery. Lumber loads are delivered by flatbed truck, which lifts up and slides the load to the ground. Naturally there will be some damage to the wood, but that is an expected part of delivery.

The Importance of Dry-In

Aside from the fact that working in a dry space protected from the elements is more comfortable, achieving dry-in is especially rewarding for the homeowner because it means that those parts of the house that are not being remodeled are finally safe from the weather.

It takes a lot of time, effort, and expense to protect an open home during construction. While this task is the sole responsibility of the HGC, that doesn't mean that you'll personally have to do the work. You'll just have to pay someone else to do it. However, you don't hire someone just for that one job. Re-securing tarps at the end of each day, and then removing them the next morning so that construction can resume, should be built into your contracts with your framing or demolition contractors and anyone else who is working on your home when it's open to the elements.

Any supplies needed to protect your home should be secured by you or purchased through your subcontractors. In my case, I bought tarps and ropes, "borrowed" an old front door to be used during my project so that my regular door would not be damaged, and purchased scrap plywood to place in window openings until the windows were installed.

Whole-House Tarps. If you plan on tearing off your roof, it makes sense to invest in a large whole-house tarp and thick, strong rope. Then, ask your framing contractor to use it. Expect that the time it takes his workers to secure the tarp and remove it will be included in his hourly rate. This could be 1 to 2 hours of extra time per day. Your framing crew is the best resource for tying down tarps, especially on a rooftop, as they're typically comfortable with heights and know how to secure the tarp to prevent it from flying off in a windstorm.

MASTER BEDROOM: We wanted a tray ceiling, concealed lighting, and distinctive trimwork in the bedroom.

Because grommets will pull out in a windstorm, and a flapping tarp can cause serious damage to yours or a neighbor's home, it's best not to use the grommets to tie down your tarp. Instead, wrap your tarp around a strong, heavy object, such as a stack of 2x4s, and then tie it with rope to securely fasten it.

Learning Curve

The Zen of Home Remodeling

Of all the challenging times we experienced during my project, I can honestly say that a night where I lay sleepless, worried, and regretful was the worst. That was the night we had one of the season's most powerful storms—right after we had torn off the roof. What would happen to the hardwood floors that I hoped to salvage in the living room? What about the rest of the kitchen and the—gasp—cabinets?

The storm lasted about a week, with torrential rains throughout. There were inch-deep pools in the living room. Water poured through the can lights in the kitchen ceiling and down onto the bubble-wrapped stove. Luckily for us, it missed the cupboards.

The framer had promised dry-in within two weeks. It actually took five weeks of mostly rainy days.

The first day back on the job, I stopped ranting and lamenting. I swept as much water off the floor as I could every day and hung around at quitting time to ensure the tarps were secured for the night.

Curiously, after a certain point, you have nothing more to fear. Things just are as they are, and you have to deal with them. But you'd also be surprised by how resilient a hardwood floor can be. After all it went through, the living room floor survived—and so did we.

Construction Drawings

At least once every day, and often more frequently than that, your construction subcontractors will need to check your working plans. It's your job to provide them with a single copy that is available to everyone. This document, which basically lives on the job site, will get pretty beaten up. Later, after your remodel is complete and you're resting comfortably in an armchair by the fire, this tattered, stained, and wrinkled copy will easily be one of your favorite souvenirs.

As work progresses, there may be small changes in how things are built. Any change to the plan should, of course, have your prior approval before it's accomplished. When any change is made, it needs to be noted on your plans so that all the other subcontractors will know what has been modified. It's important that only YOU write down these changes. No one else should be allowed permission to do so.

A Record of Construction. As you've probably surmised, this copy of your plan will become the "as built" version. As time goes on and many more changes are made—and subsequently documented—this particular set of plans will become the most accurate and valuable record of your home's construction. Keep it in a tube. Don't leave it out in the rain, let it blow off the roof, get lost, or anything else that can happen if you or your workers aren't paying attention. In addition to these best efforts, keep a backup copy of the original plan with you in your car at all times.

Each evening, your subcontractor(s) should return the plans to a pre-established location for safekeeping. They already know how important your plans are—but you need to specify where they are to be kept and instruct them to keep them safe. You will also have the responsibility of checking to see that your plans are stored properly each day. Keep the tube with the plans inside in a location, such as a stud bay, where everyone can find them.

Keep your working plans safe and dry by storing them in a 3- or 4-inch PVC tube with end caps.

Always keep a copy of your construction drawings on site. You and your subcontractors will refer to them frequently.

Minutia Matters

It's surprising that something as small as one inch or a single screw can make a difference. But in construction, it can.

For instance, when the custom screw that came with your shower drain gets lost and has to be special-ordered, your tile setter's work might be delayed an entire week. (You can't build the shower pan and set tile until the drain is securely fastened first.)

Another "tiny" detail might be that one of your new bathroom walls is only 14 inches away from the newly installed sewer pipe, making it too close to the wall to actually set the toilet once the drywall is installed. So, now you'll have to move the new wall. You get the picture.

When your subcontractors complain about what might seem to be a minor concern, pay attention, and try to understand the implications. Your construction schedule can be derailed by the small stuff.

BASEMENT APARTMENT: We planned on a basement apartment. This is one of the bedrooms.

What's Your Management Style?

It's tempting to approach your remodeling endeavor as you would a popularity contest. After all, you don't want to lose people because you're unlikable. Resist this urge. Managing your remodel is a job, and you've assumed a specific role—the role of the boss. Your workers and contractors are professionals, not friends. If you keep your discussions focused on the work ahead of you and don't use your position to blather on endlessly (you wouldn't believe how many subcontractors complain about homeowners who do this), most folks will come to respect you and your word. They might even start to like you. You also have to know what you want, so that others have the chance to earn your praise once they've accomplished it. This requires courage and a willingness to state your needs clearly and honestly. The more relaxed you are about this, the more comfortable everyone else around you will be.

Get comfortable with expressing your expectations for the performance and quality of the work.

Ask Questions. You should also get used to asking questions. In fact, asking questions and polling your professional resources to help you understand a situation is the best way to decide what should be done. Relying on their knowledge, insight, and concerns to weigh your decisions will not only lead you to better outcomes but also result in their greater commitment to your project. When you bring them into a situation in a way that makes them accountable for its outcome, they help you create the solution.

Don't ask, "What should I do?" Ask, "What's your experience with this sort of thing, and how have you handled it in the past?"

Once construction is underway, be prepared to make decisions quickly and within a limited time frame to keep your project on schedule.

Bring Treats. Another secret to success lies in the power of the DONUT. Yes, it's that simple. When you see your workers slaving away, splurge a little and get them donuts. They'll appreciate that you've noticed their efforts. This one simple act, applied judiciously, will smooth your construction project and quite possibly make your own day better, too.

Visits to the Job Site

Your subcontractor will develop a list of questions to be resolved during your scheduled visits. But you'll also get a good idea of how the job is going by simply showing up unannounced.

The subcontractors you hire should know that you expect quality work done on schedule.

TYPICAL DAILY TASKS

A HOMEOWNER GENERAL CONTRACTOR has a number of tasks to accomplish each day. If you can't name 10 things right off the bat, keep reading. Each day of work will present its own share of fires to put out, but these are the basics:

- Checking in at the job site each morning to make sure your work crew starts on time.
- Monitoring actual progress against your time lines to ensure that the construction schedule is being met (or exceeded).
- Calling upcoming contractors to confirm their start dates and times and scheduling hand-off meetings.
- Inspecting work and taking measurements.
- Comparing completed work against your blueprints to see that all the dimensions and features are correct. (Remember: minutia matters.)
- Troubleshooting with your contractors to resolve issues and answering questions that come up. These might include whether you want your stairs to be built for carpeting or for hardwood—and whether or not you plan to install a stair skirt because there are different building requirements for each.
- Talking with tile setters and other craftsmen to review how things will be laid out, and how that will affect the overall design.
- Running to the store to pick up incidental hardware, extra paint, a few pieces of lumber, or whatever is needed to keep your workers focused and productive.
- Scheduling and attending local building department inspections.
- Writing checks for materials and workers.
- Finding resources for gaps—whether it's hiring a local handyman to do general work on-site, special ordering an item, making arrangements for general cleanup, moving or removing materials, etc.
- Keeping track of the on-site copy of the plans.

Even the most timid homeowner holds the power of approval. Every time you visit or review the work, your contractors are holding their breath, waiting for your assessment. Is it good? Are you happy with their progress, the quality, their workmanship? Set the tone for your conversations with your contractor by first noticing something to appreciate. Look carefully, ask questions, and listen. After that, you can more successfully bring up and talk through any concerns.

Repeated confrontations with your workers, even over small issues, will adversely affect their morale and ultimately the quality of your remodel.

Pick Your Battles. Building, as I've mentioned before, is a creative process. While straight, even, and level aren't negotiable, your workers deserve the opportunity to apply their creativity. So listen to their suggestions and be prepared to discuss them. That's the part of their work that keeps them happy. Besides, the ideas they have could help improve your project.

Expect Changes. Once your project is underway, it's important to continually talk with your subcontractors about what's coming next so that you can stay on top of the project. Don't assume that the original progression of work that you first developed will be executed flawlessly. All sorts of things can come up that might change how you and your team approach and complete individual tasks. In order to keep a semblance of a schedule and get anything done, you have to continually revise your approach.

Handoffs between Contractors

Immediately after you've paid and released a subcontractor and are ready to begin the next phase with a different subcontractor, you learn from the new subcontractor that the work done by the previous subcontractor is

A: Not right
B: Incomplete
C: Unacceptable

The end result is that your follow-on subcontractor will not, or cannot, begin his work, and your project will come to a standstill. You can avoid all of this by understanding the sequence of work and bringing your upcoming subcontractors to the job site before they're needed to have them review and approve the foundation that they will rely upon for their own job. You can also expect that those pesky gaps I've mentioned before—things no one has thought of, or even realized (including your professionals)—will now require you to spend more money and hire additional resources. While this is a painful pill to swallow, you'll at least have some "heads up" time if you're doing a good job of sequencing work and managing handoffs.

> In construction, mistakes and omissions most often show up in the transition from one subcontractor to the next.

Managing Changes

Change is not something that you should accept easily or lightly. However, sometimes what looks good on paper turns out to be a bad idea. In those rare cases, in-field modifications or redesign (and sometimes reengineering, with more building department permitting) may be required.

That said, keep in mind that flexibility and the ability to leverage advantages—in the form of reduced costs or the elimination of a feature that seems excessive—is sometimes the appropriate course of action.

Change Forms. When a proposed change will incur additional costs, make it only if it is due to unforeseen circumstances or if the original plan, once implemented,

would be completely unacceptable to you. Before you agree to the change, make sure you understand its implications to your workers. This includes evaluating the costs of materials, time, and resources. When the change is approved, use a change-order form. While this seems like a bother, it will save you and your subcontractors later hassles by clarifying, on the front end, what exactly will be included in the new work, what it will cost, and who is doing what.

If by now you're thinking, "what a pain," you'd be right. That's exactly what it is. Avoid it wherever and whenever possible. You have enough juggling to do without adding lots of changes.

Roof trusses, opposite, are attached to a completely framed sidewall.

Kitchens, above left, are complex rooms with many interconnected elements. Keep changes to a bare minimum.

A mini-laundry, above, located near the bedrooms is a convenient, time-saving feature.

Stick around long enough and you'll hear ...
"Your money is your hammer."

Paying Subs and Suppliers

Your relationship with your subcontractors is like a marriage. The expectation of perfection never works. Ultimately, your ability to complete your remodel as intended is based on a series of successful transactions. In exchange for your money, your contractors will work on your behalf.

When it comes to having work done on their homes, most homeowners are fearful of being fleeced. Every year, the local news features at least one story about a construction scam of one sort or another. While this is a possibility, it's unlikely to happen if you've done your homework and manage your workers fairly.

These same fearful people will tell you that the way to manage subcontractors is to simply withhold money. While it's true that you should only be paying for work that's complete and properly done, you need to be fair and mindful of the work and payment schedule you agreed to in your contract. And the truth is, real life is not so simple.

So keep your business head; don't lose your cool; and actually manage your workers. That means working with them in a productive way so that you get what you want done. You can't shut down the process by withholding their livelihood.

Confirm permit sign-offs with the building department before you make the final payment to your subcontractors.

Include furniture, artwork, and personal momentos, left, in your original plans.

The master bedroom, opposite, is awash in natural light from windows on three sides of the room.

HOW TO PAY SUBCONTRACTORS

HOW YOU TALK ABOUT AND DISBURSE YOUR MONEY becomes critically important—not only from a relationship perspective, but also from a legal standpoint. Here are some basic tips for paying subcontractors:

- Pay according to the payment schedule you've included in your contract. If you dispute their work, withhold only as much money as is reasonably fair to cover the portion that is incomplete or incorrectly done. If you do withhold money, provide an explanation in writing to your subcontractor on why the money was withheld, with clear instructions on what needs to be done to get payment in full. If possible, include a fair time line for when you'd like the work completed.

- Ask for (or write up) a written receipt every single time you make a payment to a subcontractor, regardless of the method of payment. (By check, cash, or in gold bullion ...) Handwritten receipts are fine. If you write up the receipts on behalf of your subcontractors, make sure that you create two copies, and have both signed when they accept the money.

- Keep copies of all your correspondence to subcontractors and all signed payment receipts.

- If your workers leave or work performance becomes poor, don't waste valuable time. Contact a real estate attorney specializing in construction, and let them advise you on how to proceed.

CHAPTER 7

MANAGING GENERAL CONSTRUCTION

Knowledge Is Power

As the HGC, you must know enough about construction to manage the project. You may not become an expert on the subject, but you need to know enough to evaluate the work of the experts—the subcontractors you have hired. Whether your project is small or large, if you know exactly what to expect before work begins, you'll be a more successful, effective, and confident manager. The information in this chapter describes the typical stages of residential construction up to the drywall phase in the interior. Finish work is discussed in Chapter 8.

Excavation and Foundations

Excavation is just one piece in a series of preliminary construction steps that provide a foundation for home improvements. It encompasses everything from expanding your foundation to reworking the surrounding landscape, installing new facilities, and returning the ground to a level surface again.

A good excavator who is familiar with remodeling work is worth his weight in gold. Over-excavate, and you'll end up with a hole that you'll need to refill with soil, for which you will pay by the truckload. Under-excavate, and the work will have to be done twice. It makes sense to find an excavation professional who is also experienced in performing several functions, including foundation and footing work, catch-basin installation, and sewer trenching.

Most excavators provide their own equipment and charge by the hour. You'll need to make sure that heavy equipment can reach the work area.

Potential Problems. Excavation opens the door to a whole host of things to consider. Rain, runoff, and mud are issues that you'll need to address. Keep your job site clean, and reduce dust and mud by laying straw over exposed soil. In some cases, your local building department may also specify temporary erosion and sediment control requirements as part of your permit approval. Soil testing for things such as radon gas or unstable soil may be required, which will add unforeseen costs to your project. Often, it's not until the foundation or trenches are dug that problems such as an underground spring, an archeological artifact, or some other issue may arise.

It is difficult to calculate costs for this work. Even an experienced general contractor can lose money here. But preparing the ground properly and building the foundation are among the most critical pieces of your project.

The excavation contractor will bring his own equipment, but you have to provide a route for heavy machinery.

Don't forget: before digging occurs, make sure all underground utilities have been surveyed and flagged.

PROTECTING FOUNDATIONS

THERE ARE THREE STEPS to protecting a new foundation and footings from water damage.

- **Apply a "gray wall" membrane** on the exterior of your foundation walls after they have cured. This rubberized, paint-on product seals the exterior of the outside wall and prevents water penetration. The sealant should be applied on the exterior side, up to the point where the wall meets ground level. Don't apply it above ground level because it will be unsightly.
- **Install footing drains.** Footing drains consist of a perforated pipe and a filter fabric sleeve surrounded by free-draining pea gravel.
- **Add a drainage mat** to the exterior of your foundation walls. These mats wick water away from the wall and direct it down to your footing drain.

Foundations

Most homeowners don't give a second thought to the slope or elevation of their property. It's not much of an issue unless you plan to expand your home outside of its existing boundaries. When an architect prepares your plans, he'll include elevation information and specify the height of your foundation walls (also known as stem walls) as part of the plan. However, it is not uncommon for an architect to miscalculate that height.

> Once foundation work begins, perform a site evaluation with your concrete contractor to make sure that the new foundation walls are set to the proper height, which is determined by the elevations of the site itself.

Your concrete contractor will establish the exact location for your foundation, and set the elevations for your foundation walls and finished floor using the elevation control point, which is listed on your site plan. An elevation control point is a fixed reference marker within the local landscape—for example, the top of a fire hydrant—from which site measurements are taken.

By building walls based on actual site conditions, you'll ensure that your wall heights provide the proper ground clearance needed for framing. Be aware that because your concrete subcontractor bids your project on the amount of concrete used, additional height can add cost to your project.

Additional Labor. With the exception of the footing-drain trench, which can be dug by your excavator, the application of a foundation sealant and drainage mat will usually not be included in a concrete, plumber, or excavator contract. For this work, look for hourly hired help. Plan to be on-site to supervise and inspect the work to ensure that it's done properly.

Managing Downspouts. Water that runs off your roof during a downpour, hits a splash block, and then pools on the surface of the ground around your home's foundation will be a problem—if not immediately, then very soon after your remodel is complete. Because of this, downspout lines must also be considered as part of your surface-water management system. Direct their runoff to footing drains or another closed system.

Foundation Slabs. Not only should you be concerned with the stability and integrity of the slab (basement floor) itself, but you must also make sure that whatever goes under or up through the slab is installed before concrete is poured. This means that you may be interspersing your slab work with the work of plumbers, electricians, in-floor heating contractors, or other trade professionals.

Once all subslab components, including plumbing lines and electrical conduit, are in place, the concrete contractor will prepare the ground. To prevent water and water vapor in the soil from seeping up through the floor, your contractor will install and compact a 2-inch layer of free-draining granular fill. Over that, he will install a layer of 6-ml. polyethylene.

When an in-floor heating is specified, there may be multiple concrete pours. Generally, one layer of

A typical block or poured foundation requires the application of a waterproof sealant, opposite.

Learning Curve

Handling an Inspection

One of the first inspections we had was for our side sewer pipe that connects the city sewer to our house. Naturally, we were nervous. Our concerns were heightened when we learned that the plumber couldn't be there with us, and that we would have to handle the inspection ourselves. The plumber waved off our concerns, telling us that the upcoming inspection would be a "piece of cake."

So the inspector arrived. He said our new side sewer would last the next 100 years, passed us, and then asked for the drawings of the sewer so that he could record them. *What?*

As it turns out, sewer lines are part of your property's permanent record. Lucky for us, he was patient with a pair of nervous homeowners. Together we measured the sewer lines and their placement on the property. He recorded the information to document the new layout in the city records.

The moral of the story? The local building inspector is there to help. Chances are good he'll give you sound advice and be patient with you through the process. Oh, and one more thing—if you rework your side sewer, have the plumber create the plans before the inspector arrives.

the slab is poured, the in-floor system is laid, and then a second layer of concrete is installed so that the in-floor system is sandwiched in the center of the slab.

Retrofitting Foundations. Your concrete contractor will use epoxy and dowels to join new foundation walls with existing ones. Try to include the required retrofit work into your concrete contractor's contract so that any seismic requirements are completed as part of the foundation work.

To finish up, the contractor will backfill the trench around the foundation walls. Make sure that you have 8 inches or more of clearance between wood siding and ground level.

Framing

By buying your own lumber you'll save the 20- to 30-percent markup and delivery costs that your framer would naturally include in his contract. With a large project, you'll likely need a framing-hardware package. Because different framers prefer different types of hardware and usually work with a favorite supplier, have your framer prepare the hardware-package list, and then purchase these materials yourself from his supplier. The benefit of using his resource is that if an unforeseen need for a particular piece of hardware arises, the supplier will find it and provide same-day delivery free of charge.

Money-Saving Idea. Prior to any building, ask the framer to look over the lumber take-off to see if anything is missing. By catching errors before the lumber is dropped, you'll save the trouble of making the trip yourself or the cost of an additional delivery.

If your remodel includes several new doors or windows, it's also a good idea to provide your framer with a copy of that take-off, too, which will provide helpful information on window and door swing and appearance.

For a large project, you'll want to use a framing subcontractor who will provide a team of three people, one of which should have master-carpenter experience.

Good framing is evident in the straightness and levelness of your walls, ceiling, and floors. But framing—joist layout in particular—also affects your lighting and mechanical systems. Coordinate several site visits for those subcontractors during framing to make sure that the framing accommodates installation of subsequent systems and features. Remember that these systems are often designed in the field while framing is underway.

On remodeling projects, the framer must often combine new framing with existing walls and floors, left.

Check the rough openings of all doors and windows, above, during framing to make sure that what you ordered will fit properly.

Straight, flat walls, opposite, start with a framing contractor who does good work.

DOUBLE-CHECK FRAMING

FRAMING HAPPENS FAST. It's a very visible construction phase in which a lot of progress can be seen in a single day. While this is exciting and fun, don't forget to do your job and check your framer's work.

Use a level to check corners and string lines to ensure that walls are straight. Also check critical dimensions, such as window and door openings, to ensure that they're built to the exact dimensions listed on the plan. These openings will be marked with the acronym, RO (Rough Opening). Measurements for new windows and doors are based on RO size.

As you build up, look at the height of your new windows to make sure that they're positioned in the wall where you want them. While the original location of the windows in my remodel looked good on the plan, when it came to building, they felt too low and provided a less-than-satisfactory view. They had to be adjusted.

Framing Practices. In general, your framer will work from your construction drawings and build from the ground up, creating the floor system first, then the exterior walls, interior walls, the next floor, and so on.

Because remodels involve a pre-existing home, the levelness of your existing floor is a critical factor in how much additional framing work will be required. In any case, expect that there will be some unforeseen framing required in your project. An experienced remodeling framer is capable of tackling remodeling integration issues in the field and will typically build some allowance for this into his contract.

Unless you've advised your architect otherwise, your construction plans are drawn for standard plumbing fixtures. If you've ordered an extra-large bathtub after your plans are drawn, you'll need to let your framer know so that he can make adjustments to accommodate it.

Framing for Windows and Doors

The standard way to frame windows and doors is to use two-bys to frame the opening. As the HGC, it's your job to specify how you want each doorway and window to look within the wall. If you have the doorway framed too close to the adjacent wall, you won't have clearance between that wall and the door trim. In essence, the doorway (with trim) will look shoved against the wall.

The same thing can happen with windows. If you plan to use wide trim, be sure that you have accounted for the additional space around all of your windows and doors. When there are two windows next to each other, let your framer know how much trim space you want between the windows, then make sure that he carries that dimension forward to any other window pairs so that your trim size remains consistent throughout your home.

To all of your trim measurements, add the depth of drywall, which will be anywhere from ½ to ¾ inch.

Who Installs Windows? One of the issues you will face with windows is whether your framer or your window manufacturer installs them. Installation by the window manufacturer will be more expensive. However, if your framer does this work, he must install them per the manufacturer's specifications so that the warranty will remain in effect. This means you'll need to talk to your framer about your expectations and his responsibilities for the installation. To protect your warranty and make sure your framer understands this work, set up a meeting between yourself, the framer, and the manufacturer's representative. This ensures that your framer understands the window product and installation requirements and assures the manufacturer that you are installing per specifications. If there is any question later, you will have proof from the manufacturing representative that you did the work as specified.

Part of your job as the HGC is to check the quality of your subcontractors' work. Here I am checking a framed wall with a standard framing square.

As the HGC, you will need to provide—at your own expense—the additional installation materials for your framer. This mainly consists of flashing and off-the-shelf window wrap. These materials are installed, per manufacturer instruction, around window openings to waterproof them prior to installation.

Raceways and Soffits

In some cases, your electrical contractor, mechanical systems contractors, or plumber may ask your framer to create framed structures, which they'll use to house things such as cables, pipes, and heating ducts. "Raceway" is the term used for wiring. Unlike a soffit, which extends out from a wall, raceways reside within the framed wall. Soffits are used as architectural features, as in the case of coffered ceilings, or to house lighting, mechanical systems, or pipes when space within a wall or ceiling is unavailable.

Wall and Floor Framing

As mentioned, manufactured I-joists are a great choice for flooring. They're straight, strong, and all the same size, which makes for a flat, squeak-free floor. But another cause of floor squeaks occurs if the subfloor is not properly attached to the joists.

Often a framer will glue the floor down first, with a plan to return later to nail. Because the glue has already dried, the nailing will not be as tight. Over time, as the floor is walked on and the glue weakens, it will squeak.

Before signing off on wall framing, inspect to see that all of the studs within the wall are even, not warped, and ready for drywall. Depending upon how much crowning, wane, or warping there is, you may need to shim certain areas to create a more even surface for drywall. It's probably cheaper to use a general carpenter or handyman to shim walls for drywall than to have the framer do it.

Back Framing. Most framers don't have the time or inclination to include a significant amount of back framing in their contracts. This work involves adding lumber within stud bays to support structures such as towel racks, stair railings, and wall-mounted TVs. If this isn't included in your framing contract, expect to pay extra for it or find an alternate resource, such as a handyman/carpenter.

Do not release your framer from the project (or pay him in full for the back framing portion of work) until the drywall phase is complete. Additional back framing may be required to support drywall application once that work begins.

Walls and floors conceal a variety of elements that help your house function, including chases for plumbing pipes and raceways for electrical wiring.

Make sure that your framer both glues and nails the subfloor down, and that this work happens simultaneously so that no gaps can form between the joist and the substrate as the glue dries.

Custom Framing. As a newbie to general contracting, expect that your management skills will be well tested in this area. While your plans may show all the specifications for rooms, walls, windows, heights, etc., they may have little, if any, information on special features, such as the framing of coved or coffered ceilings, curved archways, and framing for rooms with dormers, which require additional infrastructure to accommodate drywall.

If you did your homework when you first discussed your project with your framing subcontractor, you will have already explained the need for these features, and you can reasonably expect that they will be included in your contract price—assuming, of course, that they are listed as a line item on your contract.

Framing Stairs. There are two ways to build stairs. One way is for carpeted stairs; the other is for hardwood stairs. Knowing how you want your stairs to look will determine how they should be built. If you want a carpeted surface, you will have your stairs built in a standard fashion, with subfloors that will run from wall to wall all the way up the stairwell. If you plan on covering your stairs with hardwood, you'll probably want a stair skirt. Stairways that include a stair skirt are built with a gap between the stringer and the wall (the stair does not meet the wall on either side.) This gap should be the width of the drywall combined with the width of the wood trim that will run along the wall on either side of the stairs. In addition, stairs surfaced with hardwood have an elongated tread.

Hardwood is wrapped around the lip of the elongated step and connects with the riser. Once framing begins, you will have to specify which stair-building method to use.

When your project includes a newel post for a stair railing, have your framer install the 4x4 post within the floor framing because it's impossible to securely mount the post to the floor after the fact.

Skylights and Other Rooftop Fixtures. In addition to framing doors, windows, and closet openings, you can also expect your framer to cut holes for skylights and set them on the rooftop. Unless you have a skylight manufacturer or your roofer do this work, your framer will cut holes for skylights, build the curbs (wood frames) around them to divert water, and then place the skylights on the rooftop so that the

Hardwood stairs require the installation of trimwork along the walls. Note the nosing on each step.

IN ORDER TO BENEFIT from the manufacturer's warranty for your new windows, doors, and skylights, be sure to follow their installation instructions. In general, window installation includes

- Shimming the window so that it is plumb, level, and square.

- Wrapping the window opening with a water-barrier product.
- Using low-expansion insulated foam to fill gaps between the window and the rough opening.
- Using flashing tape over all nail flanges after the window is securely nailed in place.
- Caulking.

roofer can flash and waterproof the opening. It's the roofer's job to screw your skylight in place.

Make sure that you know who will be responsible for cutting holes in your new roof for fans, fresh-air vents, HVAC, and plumbing pipe. If you ask your framer to cut the holes, either you—or your subcontractors—must provide the framer with information on where all openings will be located and the exact size of each hole. Keep aesthetics in mind and limit roof penetrations in areas of high visibility—such as the front of your roof.

Roof Trusses. Roof trusses will be brought to your home on a flatbed truck and placed with a crane. You need unobstructed access from the ground to allow for the movement of the crane.

Many homeowners forget to check in advance to determine whether a crane will fit into their yard. They then watch helplessly as their roof trusses head back to the lumberyard because there is no way to place them on the house. If overhead wires, trees, or power lines create an obstruction, then your framer, or another contracted resource, will have to carry them up by hand. Coordinate this work in advance.

Sheathing. Attaching exterior sheathing, which will be either plywood or oriented strand board rated for this purpose, helps stabilize the structure. Your local building code may call for corner bracing and have seismic requirements as well. Once your exterior walls are built and sheathed and before insulation is installed, caulk all small openings. A handyman typically manages this work. It's one of those HGC responsibilities that is easy to miss, but it's important, as it prevents insects from gaining access to the inside walls of your home; it also eliminates drafts and air leakage.

Pay particular attention to the corners of the window openings and use the recommended water-barrier product because that's where they typically leak.

Roof trusses are delivered to the site by truck. A crane lifts them into position on top of the wall framing.

When enclosed soffits are not part of the design, make sure your framer installs bird blocking under the truss overhang as part of his work.

Roofing

If you're adding a second story or bumping out the side of your home, you'll need to think about roofing and water diversion early on. Ask yourself how your project will affect your entire house and all its systems, including water runoff and drainage. For instance, if new gutters and downspouts are needed, where will the downspout water be directed? Downspouts should discharge into some type of drainage system.

Over-Framing. Make sure that your roofer discusses over-framing with your framing subcontractor at the beginning of the project. Over-framing includes the creation of crickets, which divert water around the base of chimneys and other roof penetrations. While most architectural plans will include a roof-framing plan, the need for crickets is determined on-site by the roofing contractor in conjunction with the framer. Other items that you, the framer, and the roofer should discuss include

- Date for dry-in, or when the roofing, wall sheathing, and windows and doors will be installed.
- Roofing schedule.
- Number and type of each roof penetration, including those for plumbing, ventilation fans, ridge vents, skylights, and HVAC.

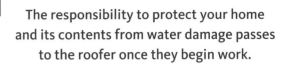

Roofing materials are dropped on the rooftop the day before roofing is scheduled to begin.

Roofers and Plumbers. All plumbing vents need to be installed through the roof before roofing, and it's the plumber's job to leave a 1- to 3-inch rubber boot, called a plumbing boot, at the job site for the roofer to install.

Next to bad weather, failure to have the proper vents, skylights, or boot materials on-site is the most common cause of roofing delays. It's your job to coordinate the

A roof in progress requires two important elements: safety equipment for the workers, such as the roof harness shown at right, and tarps for bad weather, opposite.

The responsibility to protect your home and its contents from water damage passes to the roofer once they begin work.

work, make sure that all materials are available on-site, and that the framer, plumber, and HVAC professionals have cut all holes, framed curbs, and installed pipes through the roof sheathing before the roofer arrives.

Protect Your Roof

When there are follow-on subcontractors working on your home using pump jacks and scaffolding—people doing siding, painting, chimney work, and the like—they'll want to nail their scaffolding brackets into your roof. The standard process is to lift the shingle tab at the

edge of the eave, and nail directly into the sheathing. Once work is complete, these holes should be properly sealed and caulked. This is accomplished by adding a metal flashing tab underneath the roof shingle, which is then glued down with mastic. A careless subcontractor might try to nail directly into the shingles, which will nullify any manufacturer's warranty you might be entitled to for your new roof. So the trick is to be on-site when they set up the scaffolding, and let them know your expectations.

After they're finished with their work but before they've been paid you might have to get on a ladder to determine that any holes made in the sheathing are properly sealed and caulked, and that your roof has not been damaged.

Money-Saving Idea. Your roofing costs will be considerably lower if you manage the removal and disposal of the roof through a resource other than the roofing company. Tearing off an old roof is an easy process that doesn't take specialized skills. You just pry up the shingles using a shovel or pitchfork and toss them into a construction dumpster located next to the roof so that you don't have to pick up the shingles twice. Then pull any remaining nails out of the sheathing. If you will be working with a demolition contractor, you may save some money by including roof removal as part of that contract.

Roofing Materials

Roofing can be made in a variety of materials. Simple asphalt shingles are the most common and affordable. These shingles are reinforced with fiberglass and paper and offer a lifespan of 20 to 30 years. Laminated shingles, made of multiple, staggered layers of asphalt material are also popular. They provide a more defined shadow line and more depth, color, and character to the roof.

Slate shingles are beautiful and expensive, and you will need to find a roofer who has experience working with this material. They're also three times heavier than asphalt, so you will need stronger framing and sheathing material. Other roofing options include cedar shakes and shingles, metal, terra-cotta tiles, and synthetic tiles that provide the look of slate without the expense or weight.

Have safety harness hooks installed on your roof as part of the project.

Plumbing

Basic plumbing work may involve all, or just a part of the three phases listed here.

- **Ground work** encompasses upgrades to water service or the sewer line and bringing those lines up through your slab or into the building.
- **Rough-in** includes complete installation of all piping needed behind the walls, as well as installation of drains, vents, and hose bib installations.
- **Finish** includes installation of plumbing fixtures, such as sinks, faucets, and toilets.

Because plumbers are a licensed trade, your plumbing contract may also include gas-piping work for things such as gas fireplaces, hot water tanks, gas furnaces, as well as in-floor, water-based heating systems.

Upgrading Service. If your remodel plan includes new bathrooms or a significant kitchen upgrade with additional sinks, you'll likely need to upgrade your water and sewer lines as required by your local building department. It's important to know where your water and sewer lines are located beforehand so that you and your contractor can map out where you'll tie new drains and downspouts into your existing plumbing system. Many building departments will have this information on file, and it's only a matter of visiting the office and picking up a copy of your property details.

Plumbing Materials

For water pipes, either copper or PEX, a petroleum-based plastic piping, is standard. Copper piping is expensive—and would add considerable cost to your plumbing contract. For example, in the Seattle area, a plumber might charge between $575–$600 per facility (a facility being a toilet, a sink, a spigot, and the like) when using PEX.

PEX should not hook directly into the hot water heater. The last 18 inches of pipe should be made of copper.

OVERLOOKED PLUMBING TASKS

HERE ARE SOME ITEMS to keep in mind when drawing up the contract with your plumber.

- Supply lines for ice makers
- Supply lines and drains for a kitchen island
- Pot fillers
- Pool and spa
- Hose bibs
- Mud room or dog-washing area

Plumbing fixtures are installed at the end of the project. Save money by buying the fixtures yourself.

That same project would jump to $850 per facility if residential-quality copper were installed instead.

In today's lean economy, most plumbers will try to produce a low bid for your project by using PEX, unless you request otherwise. However, if you plan to live in your home for a lifetime, consider investing in copper. PEX is a fairly new product, which means that long-term durability is not yet tested. PEX becomes brittle when exposed to sunlight and can be destroyed by rodents. The sunlight issue brings up storage concerns, and the hope that your supplier has properly housed the material before it gets to you.

Money-Saving Idea. If using copper, buy the pipe yourself. Be sure to preorder the pipe well in advance of the work so you don't hold up any plumbing work. Then store your copper in a safe place, as it's a high-theft item.

Don't forget to include plumbing for outdoor hose bibs and in-ground sprinkler systems.

Hard water erodes copper piping, so if you have hard water and you plan to use copper, consider installing thicker pipe.

Drains. The most damaging leak you can have is a drain leak. It might take months or decades to discover, but water damage to floors, ceiling, and framing almost always results in a costly fix. Drain leaks are caused by failed fittings. The more moving parts, the more likely you'll see a failure. The general contractor tip here is to avoid gasket-and-compression fittings for your drains.

Request all-glue fittings for your drains to avoid leaks, and make sure you list this on the contract with your plumber.

Ground Work

It's fairly simple to dig a new trench for your water line, which typically lies only a few feet below the surface in most areas.

Money-Saving Idea. Hire local, unskilled labor to dig your water line trench rather than making it part of the plumber's contract. Once new water lines are installed, have that same laborer fill the trench in after the work has been inspected and signed off on by your plumbing inspector.

Sewer Lines. Sewer lines will be much deeper than water lines. As a result, plan on having your excavator dig sewer trenching as part of his work. With large remodels that include significant upgrades, you might want to replace all old sewer lines to prevent later problems. There is also a requirement that sewer lines slope down ¼ inch per foot until they tie into your septic system or city sewer line. It's your plumber's job to know such requirements, along with other basic rules of the trade as defined by the plumbing code. You'll need to work out your sewer/drain line system in partnership with your team of experts, which includes the excavator, concrete contractor, sewer specialist, and/or your plumber.

If you tie your downspout drainage system into sewer lines, install p-traps in the line to prevent sewer gas from leaking out of the system and wafting into your house or yard. Nothing spoils a nice summer evening on the deck as the smell of a sewer.

Your project may require trenches for water lines, sewer lines—shown left—and perhaps, electrical utilities.

Rough-in involves running pipes through the just-framed walls, opposite left.

Rough-In

Pay particular attention to where pipes are being installed within your foundation walls. Before concrete is poured, make sure that all plumbing pipes are placed where they're supposed to be. It may be difficult to tell where the interior walls will be at this point in construction, but this is a critical responsibility of yours. Toilets, in particular, must be a certain distance from the wall to pass code. Incorrect placement could result in plumbing that doesn't fit into the room or doesn't fit into the wall properly. In this case, you would have to break up the concrete, move pipes, and then patch the slab. Another solution requires changing the room size and adjusting the interior walls during framing to accommodate your plumbing.

Wherever you have pipes running along a wall or ceiling within an interior room, make sure that you wrap them with insulation to mute the sound of running water.

MASTER BATHROOM: Our dream bath includes a large shower with multiple showerheads.

Location, Location, Location. Pay attention to the location of the water heater. If the heater is in the basement and your master bath is on the second floor, you'll have to run the water for quite a while each morning before the hot water from your tank reaches the shower. Besides the annoyance, it's wasteful. The solution is to include a hot-water recirculation system in your plumbing system. Your plumber can easily include the additional ½-inch loop of pipe during rough-in and then install a pump on your hot water tank that includes a timer so that the recirculation system automatically carries hot water to your shower at predetermined times.

Insist upon quarter-turn angle stops (ball valves) on all supply lines and the water main shutoff. These valves are durable, reliable, and stem the flow of water quickly and easily.

Today's green builders are also adding hot-water recovery systems on bath and shower drains. In addition to lowering plumbing permit costs, these systems reduce water heating costs by using heated waste water to warm the hot water tank before that water is passed out through the sewer system.

Venting. Every drain requires a vent or stack. Vents prevent your toilet from creating a vacuum when it's flushed and drawing sewer gases into your home. The size of the vent is important and is based on the number and type of fixtures used. If you have an existing vent, your plumber may be able to use that in lieu of cutting a new vent in your roof. Where new vents are necessary, you, the plumber, and the framer will work together as a team to define where the hole will be cut. It's the plumber's responsibility to stub the pipe through. Your roofer will attach the rubber boot and flashing as part of his roofing work.

Use a plumber-savvy supplier to order and purchase your plumbing fixtures, faucets, drains, and the like.

Finish Work

The actual installation of plumbing fixtures and fittings comes later in the construction process. But when buying fixtures, make sure you are dealing with a knowledgeable source. An experienced sales person will help you navigate through the maze of what sink takes what type of faucet, what drain fits what type of tub, and the like. It's not uncommon to choose a particular manufacturer and finish (bronze, chrome, stainless) for your faucets, and then find out that the same manufacturer doesn't produce a matching showerhead or tub faucet. This means that you'll have to switch to a different manufacturer for everything, or install different hardware on that particular fixture. Your specialist will know compatible, comparable brands and save you hours of frustration by providing alternatives and suggestions.

Tub Problem. Pay attention to the bathtub. Getting a new tub placed can be a challenge because most plumbers will not volunteer to carry it up your stairs and set it on the frame. Work out an arrangement with the plumber before the tub is delivered. In some cases, additional back framing will be required around the tub for support and for the installation of drywall.

Once your new tub is installed, be sure to protect it by laying a sheet of plywood over it until all of the construction is complete.

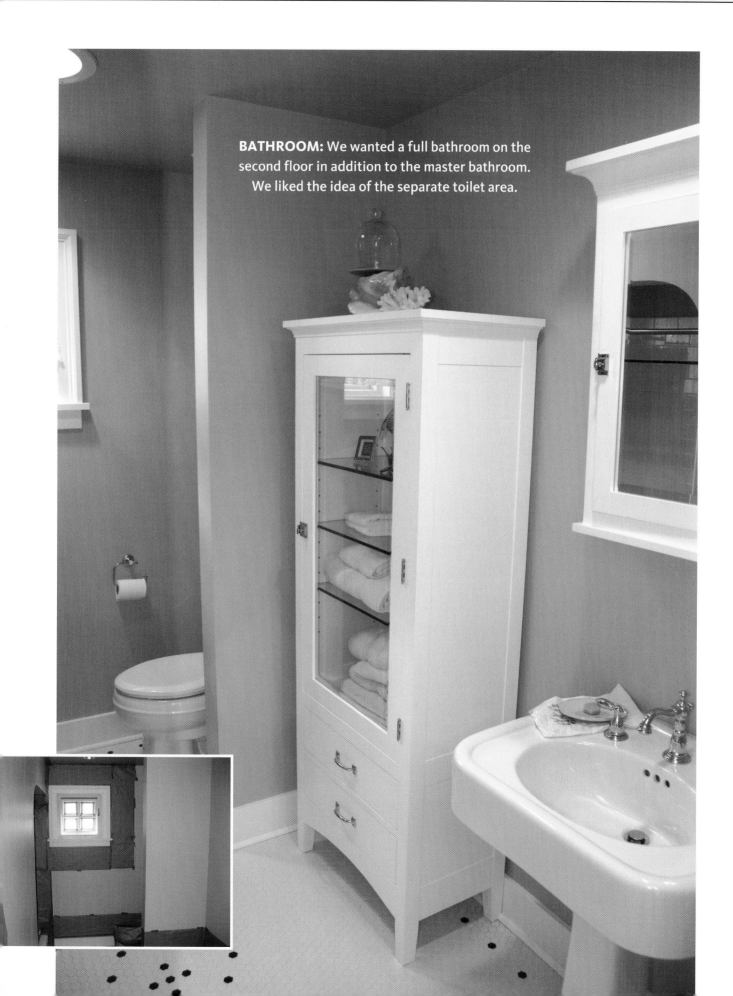

BATHROOM: We wanted a full bathroom on the second floor in addition to the master bathroom. We liked the idea of the separate toilet area.

Heating, Ventilation, and Air Conditioning

In general, the installation of HVAC systems is a complicated sequence of work with lots of overlap in terms of which subcontractor performs which tasks. Your job is to coordinate everyone's effort and make sure that all the individual tasks are delegated to the right person. HVAC involves heat and air-conditioning systems, hot water heaters, gas piping, fireplaces, exhaust fans, dryers, ranges, bathroom fans, and ventilation systems (including heat-recovery ventilators and energy-recovery ventilators).

With mechanical system installations, you must assign responsibility for individual tasks and permits.

The following examples provide an overview of tasks and transitions that must be managed by the homeowner general contractor with several types of installations. This is only a partial list to give you an idea of what to expect.

- **Gas fireplace insert:** the HVAC contractor provides ducting, the electrician installs wiring, the framer cuts the hole in the roof, the roofer sets the stack.
- **Hot water heater:** the HVAC contractor sets, straps, and vents the water heater; the plumber brings in the water line; the electrician wires the unit—but if it's a gas water heater, who will install the gas line? If your plumber does this, it's your job to make sure that he understands the stringent permit and code requirements that accompany any gas work.
- **Bathroom vent fans:** the HVAC contractor installs the unit and the duct work, the electrician brings power to the fan, the framer cuts the hole in the roof, the roofer sets the vent fixture, electrician returns to connect the fan to the wiring system.

In all cases, be sure to clarify whether you'll be purchasing and delivering the item to be installed, or if your subcontractor will be providing it through your contract

with him. Take time to have comprehensive discussions with your subcontractors for each mechanical system you install so that all tasks can be assigned and then completed per code. It also makes sense to have a handyman around on-site during this work so that construction flows smoothly.

In a remodel, mechanical systems are always custom designed.

HVAC Equipment

Heating and air-conditioning systems can dramatically change your design if you have not accommodated them to some degree in your original construction drawings. As with other construction specialties, you will provide your blueprints to your HVAC subcontractor during the bid phase to get pricing on the project. As part of that

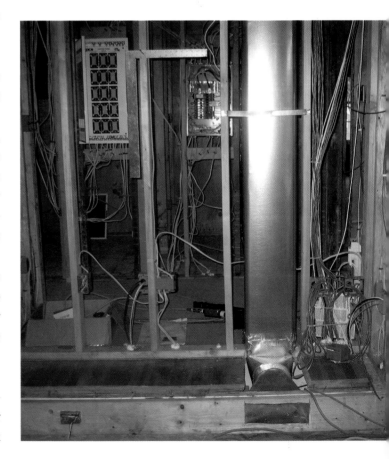

process, you and your subcontractor will establish on paper where the heating or air-conditioning systems should be located, and the route of the ducting. That initial design will be developed as you and your HVAC subcontractor walk through your home BEFORE demolition and construction starts.

Planning Ahead. However, because HVAC design or layout sometimes involves modifications to framing or other structures, ask your HVAC subcontractor to visit the site again in the later stages of framing. Together you'll walk through and identify the path for these systems, evaluating floor-joist patterns and determining where beams or other structures that might block or inhibit duct work are located in order to finalize a layout that best suits your remodeled space.

Assume some modifications to your original design, and be prepared for a few change orders to accommodate any improvements that result from your walk through. Be sure to consider how the change will impact your budget and the work of other tradespeople.

HVAC ducts and flues run inside walls and floors, opposite and above. For future reference, photograph all in-wall components before the walls are closed up and drywalled.

Money-Saving Idea. You can save considerable money on ducting material and on the need for soffits by designing your HVAC system starting from the return air grill. You'll then work backwards to the furnace location. To ensure even temperatures and efficient air filtering, install one return air grill on each floor. Place register vents near a doorway or window to increase airflow.

One final note about heating register vents: pay attention to where your heat vents are located within a wall so that they do not interfere with trimwork, causing extra finish-carpentry work or the need for custom vent covers.

> Because your plumber and your HVAC contractor both have roof venting requirements that need to be handled by your framer, coordinate a meeting between them at the job site to finalize stacks and ducts.

Money-Saving Idea. It's often difficult to decide which company to use when it comes to installation of gas-powered water heaters, fireplaces, or in-floor heating systems. Trust that whenever you purchase installation from a retail store, you will pay dearly for it. You'll save money by using the experts on your own construction team. Both your plumber and your HVAC subcontractors may have gas-line installation expertise, as well as in-floor heating system experience. As you weigh your options, remember that your goal is to find a resource that will provide the best recourse if something goes wrong. Depending upon the size of the project, you might be better off choosing a specialized subcontractor—especially for something like a large in-floor heating system.

Water Heaters. Options include electrical, gas, solar, and—for those with reduced space—tankless water heaters. Different water heaters have different installation and location specifications. Be sure to check requirements in advance and identify who among your construction team will be installing the unit.

Electrical

Depending upon where your electrical service comes into your home, you may need to have your service temporarily moved by a licensed electrical contractor before construction begins.

As with plumbing, there are three phases to electrical work in a large remodel project:

- **Ground Work.** This includes relocation of electrical service and/or running wire from the service box to areas outside of the home, such as to a detached garage.
- **Rough-In.** This includes running wiring within the home, setting junction boxes for switches and outlets, and all circuit-panel work.
- **Finish Work.** This is completed after all painting work is done and includes the mounting of fixtures, switches, and outlet plates.

> You'll need a minimum of two circuits with ground-fault circuit interrupter protection at the job site to accommodate power tools and other construction activities.

Plans and Permits

Electrical planning includes everything from interior lighting to garden fountains and everything in between, including appliances, hot tubs, furnaces, sound systems, security systems, alarms, generators, doorbells, telephones, computer equipment, and exhaust fans. The important thing to remember, no matter how large or small your project, is that the best time to upgrade the electrical system within your home is when the walls, floors, and ceiling are open.

> The smart homeowner is thinking about pre-wiring for future needs.

In many jurisdictions, homeowners are not required to use a licensed electrical contractor or submit a formal plan for their electrical work if they plan on doing it themselves. However, permits and inspections will be required for most work, regardless of whether the homeowner performs the task or not. Check with your local building department to make sure you understand the electrical codes in your area.

If you do the electrical work yourself, draw up a formal plan. This will not only help you remember the location of all the lights, outlets, switches, and fixtures, but it will also focus your thinking around location and use so that you end up with a design that meets your needs over time.

> If your work does involve the service panel, have your electrician add voltage protection to prevent power-line voltage spikes from destroying your electronic equipment.

Don't cover anything until the relevant building inspector signs off on the work.

Electrical Considerations

Symmetry and aesthetics matter when it comes to the placement of light fixtures, outlets, and switches. Because service boxes are installed during framing when the walls are open, many people make the common mistake of placing switches and outlet boxes too close to doorways, windows, or the end of a wall where two walls intersect.

Switch and outlet boxes should be securely installed so that they don't move out of position during the drywall phase. They should be straight and placed at the right height. Also, test all of your outlets to make sure that they are live before drywall goes up so that you do not have to tear out a wall to fix a circuit after the walls are installed.

Take pictures of your wiring, plumbing, and mechanical systems while the walls and ceiling are open—and before your drywall subcontractor comes in—so that you have a record of their locations.

Electrical for a kitchen usually includes circuits devoted to lights and others for appliances. Some appliances, such as dishwashers, require dedicated electrical circuits.

Interior Lighting. As mentioned, the key is to know what you want—where lights are to be located, how you plan on using them, and what location would be most convenient for turning them on and off. While there are minimum standards for the number and location of circuits and toggle switches within different rooms, as defined by the National Electrical Code (NEC), your electrical contractor can customize your lighting design with minimal extra cost.

> Save money right off the bat by incorporating natural light into your remodel.

Get Advice from Experts at Lighting Stores. These folks can help you make excellent decisions on what to install based on the outcome that you wish to achieve. Be sure to define who is buying what in your electrical contract. Make sure that your contractor receives the items that you provide in a timely manner so that his schedule will not be slowed or stopped. For any items your electrical contractor is providing, you need a clear description (type, model number, color) and understanding of the operation of that item. For example, switches can include anything from a simple manual toggle, to a highly complex, programmable switch with multiple operations. If you want to have the programming function, you'll need programmable switches.

Recessed lights, right, are best installed while the ceiling is still open. Talk with a lighting expert to determine the types of fixtures and the spacing required for your project.

Plan on a variety of lighting sources, opposite. Our kitchen lighting plan included recessed lights, hanging fixtures over the snack bar, and under-cabinet lights for working at the counter.

Recessed Lighting. Recessed lighting is stylish and can flood the room with light, while lamps and fixtures add warmth and design impact. When it comes to purchasing recessed fixtures (cans) there is a wide variety in type and quality. Some models may require special ordering. Spotlights allow you to highlight areas and bring attention to a specific feature, such as a mantle, bookcase, piece of art, or a curio cabinet. Because recessed lighting fixtures are set between joists or stud bays, the location of the framing impacts fixture placement. In any case, recessed lights should be arranged in an orderly array. Recessed lights come in 4½-, 5-, and 6-inch widths. The size of your fixtures will dictate how many you'll need to meet code or accomplish your lighting goals. Save money by buying fixtures yourself and hiring your electrical contractor for labor only.

> Kitchens should be well lit over cooking and work areas, with the ability to dim the brightness for entertaining.

Convenience and Access. The features on power switches have come a long way since the toggle switch. With today's programmable switches you can turn on multiple lights simultaneously, either manually or by remote control, to create mood lighting, lighting for reading or TV viewing, or dining. To achieve these effects you'll need to expand your thinking beyond a single light fixture in each room or old-fashioned, manually-operated switches. In a large room, you may want two or three different lighting options. You might also consider connecting your lighting to your alarm system so that if an alarm goes off, a light comes on automatically. You can also program lights to switch on and off at predetermined times to provide security while you're away from home. High-end choices include auxiliary power systems, such as a generator, and setup for immediate or later installation of solar power. Many people predict that solar power will become an affordable option for most homeowners within the next 10 years. If you are able to install wiring for solar now, you could save big installation costs down the road if you choose to convert.

The inventor of "The Clapper" made a fortune from people who lack convenient switches for their lighting.

To figure out where you'll need electrical outlets, picture yourself in the room—vacuuming, reading, watching television, doing hobbies, or using your computer—and have outlets placed where they will provide convenient access.

Switches and Receptacles. Who hasn't struggled with putting up a string of holiday lights, only to find that the power cord must be run through an open window? Talk with your entire family about how they plan to use a particular room or area, what special needs should be met, and where the switches and outlets—what the pros call receptacles—should be placed. Left to his own devices, your electrical contractor will install the minimum number of switches and outlets in standard locations. But only you will know where furniture will eventually be placed, whether or not you'll be installing speakers within a particular room, and where spotlights are needed to highlight artwork or showcase the mantle. Before your contractor runs wire, walk through the area and identify where you want things placed. For example, in a large room, you might also want in-floor outlets so that lamps or laptops do not require extension cords to reach the receptacle.

Electrical Extras. Don't forget that toilets now include high-tech features such as bidets, warmed seats, automatic flushing, and air drying. If this sounds like something for your home—either now or in the future—include electrical service in your plan. An under-sink mounted instant hot water tank is another common feature that requires a circuit.

Have one or two GFCI outlets installed in the lower bathroom cabinets so that you can keep electrical devices, such as your toothbrush recharger, inside the cabinet.

152

Exterior Lighting. Outlets on the exterior of your home provide electricity for lawn and power tools, equipment such as pressure washers, holiday lighting, a hot tub, a fountain, or a pool. Exterior lights provide security and can also be used to add ambience to your garden, stairs, and walkways. Protect all exterior outlets with a ground-fault circuit interrupter (GFCI).

Central Vacuum. Have your central vacuum system installer coordinate hose outlet locations with your electrical contractor. Vacuum manufacturers have pre-established hose lengths, so having enough outlets in the right locations (where your hose can reach every part of your home) is key to your ability to fully use your system.

Include outdoor lighting for safety and as a design element in your landscape plan.

Phones and Network Cable. Going wireless for your phone and computer is convenient, but you should know what the trade-offs are. If you choose to wire, you'll need a specialist to install the Ethernet, which should be done at the same time that other house wiring is being done.

Smoke Detectors. According to the U.S. Fire Administration, 3,425 individuals died as a result of fire in 2006. Four out of five fire deaths occur in the home. Smoke alarms reduce the likelihood of residential fire-related fatalities by half by providing an early warning and the chance to escape. Your local building department also requires them.

Different types of smoke alarms detect different types of smoke, based on the type of the fire. Today, there are three varieties to choose from: ionization, photoelectric, and dual-technology. While all three technologies are good, the fire-safety community prefers dual-technology to ensure the most protection. Some smoke detectors can also detect carbon monoxide (CO) a toxic colorless and odorless gas that can be deadly at high levels.

- **Ionization Alarms:** quickly react to smoke caused by flames and fast-moving fires, such as a kitchen fire.
- **Photoelectric Alarms:** quickly react to smoky and smoldering fires, such as those ignited by a match or cigarette on bedding or between furniture cushions.
- **Dual-Technology (Dual-Sensor) Alarms:** contain both photoelectric and ionization sensors in one unit.

An interconnected smoke detector system will set off all of the smoke detectors in your home, regardless of where the fire is located, providing you with valuable extra time. If your project doesn't include a lot of wiring, consider adding a wireless interconnected smoke alarm system as part of your remodel. Hard-wired smoke detector systems are typically installed by an electrical contractor.

Other Systems. In the home, CO can result from open flames, gas water heaters, space heaters, or a blocked chimney. A plug-in carbon monoxide monitor will detect a problem and provide a warning.

Security systems should be coordinated with your electrical contractor and/or a professional security-system contractor.

If you're doing a full-house remodel, tie your smoke detectors into the electrical system of your home. Include at least one UL-Listed smoke alarm on every level of your home, including the basement.

In addition to lights, you will need wiring for smoke detectors, phones, computers, and the HVAC system.

Siding and Exterior Trim

Techniques for siding depend on both the area of the country you live in and the material you choose for the exterior of your home. While there are a multitude of materials to use (cedar siding, shingles, hardboard, stucco), there are some basics that apply to all. In a remodel, you will likely be integrating new siding with pre-existing siding, unless your current siding needs replacement because the contrast between old and new would be too noticeable.

Before siding is installed over sheathing, a house wrap of some sort is applied. There are a number of products used for this purpose, including roofing felts. We chose a product that provided a moisture barrier on the outside but still allowed the house to breathe.

The siding subcontractor will then apply flashing to the windows and doors. Regardless of the types of windows and doors, it's your job to confirm that either the flange or flashing provides a slight overhang over the tops of all your windows and doors before the siding is nailed on.

> When installing cedar siding wider than 6 inches, prime both the front and the back to prevent cupping—which occurs when moisture on the backside expands and contracts at a different rate than the primed front.

Exterior Trim. In addition to house wrap, flashing, and siding, your project may include exterior trim around windows and doors, and decorative trim such as a bellyband and enclosed soffits.

If you have not used an architect to map out exterior features, you'll need to spend time in the field talking with your subcontractor to identify trim type, integration work, and the like. With a good siding contractor, you'll be able to talk through a variety of solutions and choose a course of action that makes the most sense for you. However, it's unfair to expect that your siding contractor will provide you with all possible design ideas. You should have a clear picture in your mind—or in your hands in the form of a photograph or magazine picture—of what you want done, and what it should look like when completed.

Caulking. Basic caulking is generally included as part of the siding contract, unless you have money to burn—in which case you can include it in your painting subcontractor agreement. In addition, if there is a long time lag between the end of your siding contractor's work and the start of your painting contractor, and your home has not been caulked, you run the risk of possible water damage in areas where gaps remain unfilled.

You should also plan on being present on the first day your siding goes up to ensure that your siding subcontractor does not over-sink the nails. They should be flush with the siding so that indentations are not visible.

> Insist that your siding subcontractor use high-quality exterior caulk and specify the exact brand in your contract, or provide the caulk yourself.

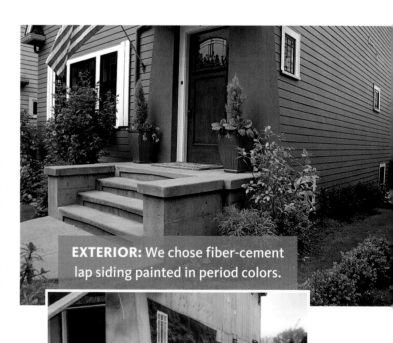

EXTERIOR: We chose fiber-cement lap siding painted in period colors.

Insulation

Unglamorous as it is, insulation is one of those construction "must haves" that provides you with two great benefits: it keeps your home-energy costs down and aids in noise reduction.

Because insulation is bulky, prickly to handle, and not that costly, it's best provided by your subcontractor as part of your insulation contract. There are no big dollars to be saved by purchasing your own insulation materials and delivering them to the job site.

As with other parts of construction, you'll need to provide your subcontractor with a clear idea of the level of soundproofing and energy savings you hope to achieve. You can then work directly with your subcontractor to develop a list of materials to be installed for your remodel as part of the bid process, or you can talk with your local utility to learn what they recommend. In either case, because local jurisdictions have specific codes on insulation requirements, and insulation must be inspected and approved by your local building department, be sure to check with them to make sure that you

Insulation cuts energy costs. And, as shown here, it also serves as a sound barrier.

are meeting or exceeding code with your final insulation plan. If you plan on exceeding the insulation levels normally found in your area, be sure to discuss any extra requirements with the framer.

Soundproofing. Your insulation contract should include wrapping water pipes and insulating bathroom walls, areas where your HVAC systems are located, rooms where sound systems will be installed, and between floors to quiet down unwanted noise. While soundproofing insulation is not required by code, it's a quality-of-life improvement that you will not regret. To save costs, this is one area where you and a friend can easily do the interior wall and pipe insulation work.

R-Values

INSULATION comes in the form of fiberglass batts, lightweight rigid panels (with or without foil), and blown-in materials—which are often used because of their ease of installation and ability to fill in oddly shaped areas.

The R-value of insulation refers to the measure of thermal resistance of the material. The higher the R-value, the better the insulation will resist heat transfer. As you evaluate what type of insulation to install in particular locations of your home, remember that insulation not only provides protection against heat or cold, but also wind. Building codes will require that you insulate all exterior walls as well as the attic space.

CHAPTER 8

MANAGING
FINISH WORK

Approaching the Finish Line

*Once the inside of your home is safe from the elements, you will begin to
see the light at the end of the remodeling tunnel. It is still some distance away because
there is a lot of work your subcontractors must complete. And there are a number
of things left for you to do, too.*

Drywall

When you budget for drywall for your remodel, don't forget the upgrades you're planning to make to existing areas of your home. New windows and doors, plumbing, electrical, and HVAC systems may also require the attention of the drywall subcontractor. This means that the drywall portion of your remodel might be considerably larger than you first imagined. It's smart to understand and plan for this from the beginning.

Avoid De-construction. However, if you haven't given it much thought, this phase of construction offers plenty of "While we're at it…" opportunities, which most homeowners find irresistible. The problem, as mentioned in earlier chapters, is that such an approach can quickly result in out-of-control costs and unintended consequences. It's a domino effect: once a wall is opened or new ones are created, you suddenly envision a structural change or system upgrade that is too good to pass up at the time.

However, such a course of action is fraught with danger because you've suddenly switched from construction—which is a forward-moving process—to de-construction—which moves your project in the opposite direction. Once the change is made, you do switch back into construction mode, but by then your costs have gone up and your schedule is in shambles. Your framer, at this point, is on to his next project, as some of your other subcontractors may be. Not only will you have to find new resources, but in your haste to get the upgrade or change made quickly, you may have skipped important planning and pre-ordering steps, as well as basics such as bidding and contracts. At this point, things start to get difficult. You have little control over your subcontractors, and your project slips into remodeling hell. Let's just not go there.

When your remodeling project encompasses more than 60 percent of the house, consider upgrading existing systems—just be sure to plan for them from the very beginning.

Alert the drywall subcontractor to special requirements, such as this eye-level recess for a TV in the master bedroom.

Types of Drywall. Drywall, also known as gypsum board or wallboard, comes in three thicknesses: ¼, ½, and ⅝ inch. In cases where fire protection is required by your local building department, a double layer of ⅝-inch drywall is applied. In general, you can rely on your drywall contractor to calculate the type and thickness of drywall needed for your project. However, know that ⅝ inch, while more expensive, will provide straighter, flatter walls with better soundproofing qualities.

Delivery Requirements. If you have a large project, talk with your subcontractor about the delivery process, time line, and—here's the important part—the opening that will be used to get the drywall into the house. Large loads will be delivered using a boom truck, and it's not uncommon to load drywall through a large window or doorway opening. In fact, it's better to keep plastic over a window opening until all drywall is delivered than to have to remove and reinstall the window.

Hanging and taping drywall is an extremely messy process. Drywall dust is one of the worst kinds of dust in the construction business. Despite all of your efforts, it will find its way into every part of your home, including furniture, shoes and clothes in your closet, cupboards, refrigerators, and the like. The floor will be quickly covered with dust and dried gobs of drywall joint compound. Instead of wasting valuable time shop-vacuuming and scraping the floor, protect it in the first place—even if it's only a subfloor.

Cover windows with plastic to prevent them from getting covered with joint compound during the drywall phase.

A Drywall Base. Because the substrate—in this case the framing—is the foundation for drywall, it needs to be level to achieve a quality outcome. Make sure that all inside corners, tub edges, and any 45-degree angles have adequate back framing. The backing stabilizes the framing and provides plenty of nailing surfaces for the drywall contractor.

Drywall is especially prone to cracking on coffered, tray, or cathedral ceilings. As the house settles, cracks sometimes form inside the 45-degree angle. With proper backing, and additional drywall at weak points, this problem is less likely to occur.

Types of Drywall Finishes. There are a number of drywall finishes available, from smooth to a variety of textures. In general, the type you choose will depend on

- The effect you want to create.

- The natural and artificial lighting in the room.

- How the new wall texture fits with the undisturbed parts of the house.

- How much maintenance you can handle.

Lay down two layers of hardboard with taped seams before drywalling begins. After the drywall is complete, it's easy to pick up and remove the first layer; your floor is still protected for the painting phase of construction.

Tray ceilings and soffits require extra framing so that the drywall subcontractor has adequate nailing surfaces.

In general, smooth walls tend to be more consistent because there is no need to match an existing texture. They are also easier to clean. But imperfections on smooth walls become obvious in sunlight and direct artificial light, especially when finished with high-gloss paint. That means if you select smooth walls for painting, they must be as perfect as possible. (See pages 160 and 161 for different levels of a smooth drywall finish.)

The desire to achieve perfection can become a cost issue. The highest-quality finishes require more materials and are more labor intensive. Costs can quickly skyrocket if you end up asking your drywall contractor to return multiple times to make the wall smoother. Avoid escalating costs by hiring an expert in the first place and choosing the right finish for each area of your home at the beginning of the project.

HOME OFFICE: We wanted office space and found it in an unused bedroom. Note the drywall taping required for this wall.

DRYWALL GRADES

THERE ARE BASICALLY FIVE "GRADES" OR LEVELS of drywall finish. The following describes each level, the amount of work involved, and the typical application for that type of drywall finish. These standards were developed by four industry groups: The Association of the Wall and Ceiling Industries International, The Gypsum Association, Ceiling and Interior Systems Construction Association, and Painting and Decorating Contractors of America. The standards are based on the final decoration planned for the room.

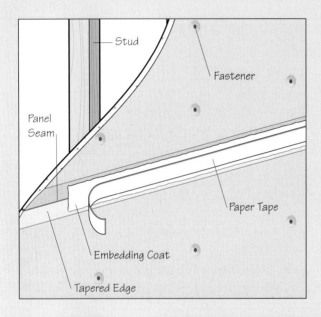

Stud
Fastener
Panel Seam
Paper Tape
Embedding Coat
Tapered Edge

Level 1

This level of drywall finish involves application of drywall, joint compound applied over all wallboard joints, and drywall tape embedded in the compound. Surfaces should be free of excess joint compound, but ridges in the compound or tool marks are acceptable. This level is also referred to as "Fire Taping" and is used when fire resistance for gypsum board is required.

Typically used for garages, attic spaces, and any concealed area.

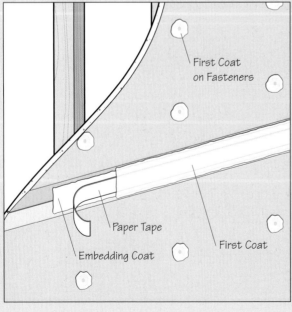

First Coat on Fasteners
Paper Tape
First Coat
Embedding Coat

Level 2

This level involves application of all the elements in Level 1, after which a layer of joint compound is added to wallboard joints, interior angles, indentations left by fastener heads, and all imperfections and recesses. Joints are then brush sanded, but tool marks and ridges are still OK.

This level is frequently used as a substrate for tile or in garages, warehouses, or storage areas where surface appearance is not a primary concern.

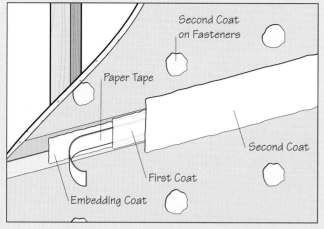

First Coat — Embedding Coat — Paper Tape — Second Coat on Fasteners — Second Coat

Level 3

This level involves the elements in Level 2 plus the application of an additional coat of joint compound over all joints, interior angles, and fastener heads. Joint compound should be smooth and free of all tool marks.

Level 3 is used as a foundation for either a final decorative texture or a heavy grade wallcovering. This level is not recommended if you want a smooth painted finish or are installing light wallcoverings. Apply a drywall primer before the final finish.

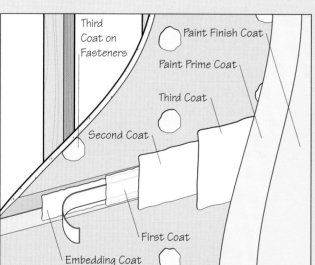

Third Coat on Fasteners — Paint Finish Coat — Paint Prime Coat — Third Coat — Second Coat — First Coat — Embedding Coat

Level 4

This level includes all the elements of Level 3 with the addition of another coat of joint compound over all flat joints and fastener heads. All joint compound needs to be smooth and free of tool marks. Care must be taken to ensure that areas of high visibility or with critical lighting are properly surfaced.

Level 4 is the most economical version of a smooth wall. It is an adequate surface for flat paints, light-texture surfaces, and wallcoverings. Prime the surface before painting. This level is not recommended for walls that will eventually be painted with gloss, semi-gloss, or enamel paints.

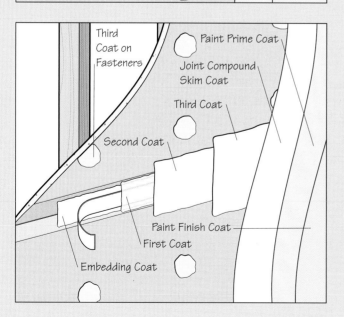

Third Coat on Fasteners — Paint Prime Coat — Joint Compound Skim Coat — Third Coat — Second Coat — Paint Finish Coat — First Coat — Embedding Coat

Level 5

This is the highest quality treatment for smooth walls. It includes all of the elements of Level 4, and then the application of one or two layers of skim coating (a thinned out version of joint compound, or one of the products that are especially designed for skimming) and sanding of all walls.

This finish accepts any sheen of paint, including high gloss and enamel. Prime the walls first. Level 5 is used in critical light areas and in homes where smooth walls are desired.

Level 5 smooth walls cost about 20 percent more than level 4.

Drywalling Conditions. Drywall requires a consistent temperature because each layer of joint compound must be fully dry before the next layer is applied. The ideal temperature is 70 degrees with low humidity. Provide electric heaters while the work is in progress. Don't use propane heaters because they add moisture to the air.

Provide a dehumidifier and fan on every floor to improve airflow. Do not fire up your furnace to keep the room warm unless you install double filters on it. Drywall dust will clog the ducts and damage the furnace.

Priming and Sealing. Priming is critical because it seals the wall to ensure that paint or the finish texture adheres evenly. In some areas, local codes require that the primer must contain a vapor barrier. Either your drywall subcontractor or your painting subcontractor can do this. However, regardless of who does the work, ask in advance what type of primer will be applied, and check the containers to ensure that the proper product is used. Sometimes, a less scrupulous subcontractor will use a mixture of old, leftover paint as a drywall primer, which spells disaster for the finish paint job.

Quality Inspection. Shine a flashlight on new drywall after it has been primed to detect imperfections; then place a small piece of blue painter's tape on the wall at the location of the imperfection to indicate where touch ups are needed.

Drywall Bids

The drywall bid (and subsequent contract) will be based on the amount of square footage covered. Specifics such as tie-ins, doorjambs, the number and type of 45-degree angles, and the like should be spelled out in the contract. Unusual requests and detail work will increase the cost. Other important points to include in the bid are

Archways and other curved surfaces require special drywall application techniques.

- Contractor will supply drywall, load the material, and install it per the Wall and Ceiling Industries International best practice guidelines.

- The drywall finish level for each area (and type of textured surface, if applicable).

- The cost and specifications for priming surfaces (if not to be done by your painter).

- A requirement covering daily cleanup (exterior and interior) and disposal of scrap.

- A requirement to clean floors by scraping and sweeping as necessary.

Expect to pay approximately $1.50–$1.75 per square foot for drywall work on a remodeling project.

HGC Job-Site Duties

- Heating (and humidifiers)
- Fans
- Power
- Water
- Sealing off rooms and covering windows
- Specifying an outdoor location where the drywall crew can clean their tools (this is a daily activity). The location should be an area where runoff will route to an approved drain system.

For a typical drywall job of three or four rooms, assume a one-person crew taking 10–15 working days. Plan on it taking a larger crew about two to three weeks for a whole-house project.

STAIRS: We wanted to add new stairs off of the front entry

Molding and Trim

At the very least, figure out the widths of the molding and trim you plan to use before the framing phase of construction begins so that doorways, windows, and mechanical systems can be framed properly.

For features such as fireplace mantles, bookcases, and built-ins, you need to select and purchase specialty or exotic woods and help your finish carpenter to finalize designs so that they seamlessly integrate with the rest of your molding and trim.

Be Consistent. Use a consistent size and style of molding or trim in adjacent rooms to maintain a cohesive feeling. For instance, if you add crown molding to a new kitchen that opens up into a great room, match the crown moldings for a more coordinated look. Don't ever discontinue a line of trim mid-span within a room.

While you don't have to apply crown molding throughout the house, make sure that baseboards, doorjambs, and window trim are uniform. There is definitely

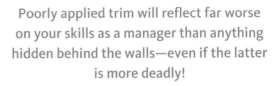

Poorly applied trim will reflect far worse on your skills as a manager than anything hidden behind the walls—even if the latter is more deadly!

an "art" to this type of work. To achieve the best results, use a professional finish carpenter who will have all the necessary tools and experience to accomplish your goals.

Money-Saving Idea. You can save both money and time in the painting phase by purchasing already-primed wood trim, molding, doors, and windows. The cost of priming trimwork far outweighs the small increase in price of preprimed materials.

Thresholds. New exterior doors typically come with a threshold that is part of the prehung door assembly. However, if you're installing an antique door in an existing or new opening, you will likely need a custom doorjamb and threshold. This is typically built in place, with the carpenter frequently referencing the new door and its dimensions to build out the jamb and threshold. It's an expensive investment, but worthwhile under the right circumstances.

Plan the type of molding and trimwork you want early in the design process. The size of the molding profiles can influence the locations of doors and windows.

Tie the design of different areas of your home together by using the same style and size of trimwork throughout, above and right.

The thresholds between rooms can also be an issue for the HGC. Where two dissimilar flooring types meet, such as between a carpeted room and a room with hardwood floors, many contractors install a prefabricated wood or metal transition strip. But you can achieve a more elegant look and avoid the need for interior transition strips or thresholds by discussing the final floor surface with your subcontractors well in advance (think bidding stage) so that seamless transitions can be built in. This work starts with your framer at the subfloor level and involves some discussion as to how each room transition will look. For instance, to create a seamless, level transition between tile and other surfaces, your tile subcontractor will need to chamfer the cut edge of the tile, using a tool called a rub stone, to eliminate all sharp edges along the transition line.

Painting

Exterior painting and caulking are, in my opinion, difficult processes that are best left to a professional. Not only do you face the elements, but you're also challenged with matching the existing paint and color if you are not repainting the entire house. There is also the matter of heights and difficult-to-reach areas.

However, interior painting is one job that many homeowners are ready to take on themselves. For those who are willing to work hard, learn about the process in advance, and invest in the proper equipment, painting can be a good way to save money. We used 19 different types and colors of paint in our project, and we saved approximately $30,000 by doing the interior painting work ourselves.

> Hold off on painting for a few weeks after drywall is installed and primed so that the walls can dry and any bubbles embedded in the joint compound have time to rise to the surface.

Quality-Control Tip. Because your paint job is only as good as the wall surface underneath, you need to thoroughly examine wall seams for bubbles or nails that have surfaced during drying. Have those areas repaired and re-primed before painting begins.

Painting also requires proper preparation and clean-up. Some claim that it's best to cover windows with plastic, using painter's tape to seal the edges. Others believe that any paint residue left on the glass can just as easily be scraped off with a razor blade once it has dried. A good rule of thumb is to cover what you don't want exposed to the paint.

Painter's Tape. Also, make sure that your painting contractor, or whomever does the interior painting work, uses professional painter's tape. It's the best product for this job, but it is not foolproof. If left in place too long or exposed to excessive sunlight or heat, even painter's tape will stick to the underlying surface. Care must also be taken when pulling painter's tape off so that if it does stick to the paint, the damage can be limited to a small area for later touch up.

Prep work, such as masking walls when spray painting woodwork, left and above, is one of the most time-consuming tasks for painters.

Color choice, opposite, can be based on what you like, as well as the furnishings you will place in the room.

Painting Sequence. A big question many homeowners ask is what to paint first when finishing a completely new area. While the sequence can vary, and different painters may have different approaches, I recommend that an initial coat of paint be applied to the walls after they've been primed and before the flooring or trim work is installed. A second coat of paint is applied either before or after trim and flooring is installed, based on the amount of trim and type of flooring that will follow. Carpeting should always be installed after painting is completed because a spill could be disastrous. However, in the case of hardwoods, vinyl flooring, or ceramic tile, painting can be completed after they're installed because these materials can be easily protected with plastic.

Interior painting is a big project, especially if you have a significant area to cover. Just to give you an idea of the scope of the work involved, the following outlines the sequence of my own interior painting project:

- Drywall primed by drywall subcontractor.
- Allow primer to dry, check for flaws, make repairs, and spot-prime.
- First coat of paint applied to walls and ceilings.
- Hardwood and tile floors installed by tile and flooring subcontractors.
- First coat of paint applied to uninstalled manufacturer-primed doors.
- Second coat of paint applied to walls and ceilings.
- Preprimed trim and moldings installed by finish carpenter throughout the house.
- Caulk, caulk, caulk.
- Second coat of paint applied to uninstalled doors. First coat of paint applied to installed preprimed trim and moldings.
- Second coat of paint applied to trim and moldings.
- Wall touch-up.
- Trim touch-up.
- Painted doors installed.

For the exterior painting, we found it best to hire professionals to do the work.

Paint Types

The paint industry is dynamic—always inventing newer, improved, and more eco-friendly products. Most homeowners will choose a simple eggshell, gloss, or flat paint (or some new hybridized version of one of them) for the interior of their home. Your local paint store or supplier will have volumes of information on the types, qualities, and applications for all of their products. Rely on them for their expertise.

Deciding what to use where, however, is the HGC's job. Flat paints are easy to touch up, but more difficult to keep clean and maintain. It's better to repaint a wall covered with flat paint than to attempt to wash it, as many flat paints will wash off the wall along with the dirt. Unless you want to touch up your walls frequently, flat paints should not be used for high traffic areas such as hallways, entrance areas, or stairwells.

Eggshell paints create an easy to clean surface, but underlying imperfections are more noticeable and walls are sometimes difficult to touch up because they develop a sheen if the area is over-sprayed.

Paint Equipment. Paint rollers come in different pile types, (smooth, medium, and rough) which leave behind a slight texture on a smooth wall. Even "smooth" rollers will leave an "orange peel" effect. If you've paid a premium for level-5 smooth walls in your home, it makes little sense to destroy the effect by using a paint roller. If you want a perfectly smooth surface, sprayers work best.

A smooth-painted finish relies on a good drywall job and attention to prepainting prep work.

Windows, Doors, and Trimwork

When your remodel includes new construction, wood trim moldings and doors are primed and painted before they are installed. After installation, all trimwork, including window and door casings, must be caulked to eliminate the gaps. Caulking is applied in corners and where the wood trim meets the drywall.

For trimwork and doors, a sprayer will provide a completely smooth surface—and will make the work go fast. You'll need a good-sized workspace to spray trimwork and doors. Using a brush will take a lot more time, and brushes can leave marks.

Avoiding Stuck Windows. If new wood windows are included in your remodel, talk with your paint-store specialist about what type of primer to use on the inside of your window frames. There is an art to painting operable windows, especially double-hung windows, so that they

Save time and money by purchasing already primed wood doors, windows, and molding.

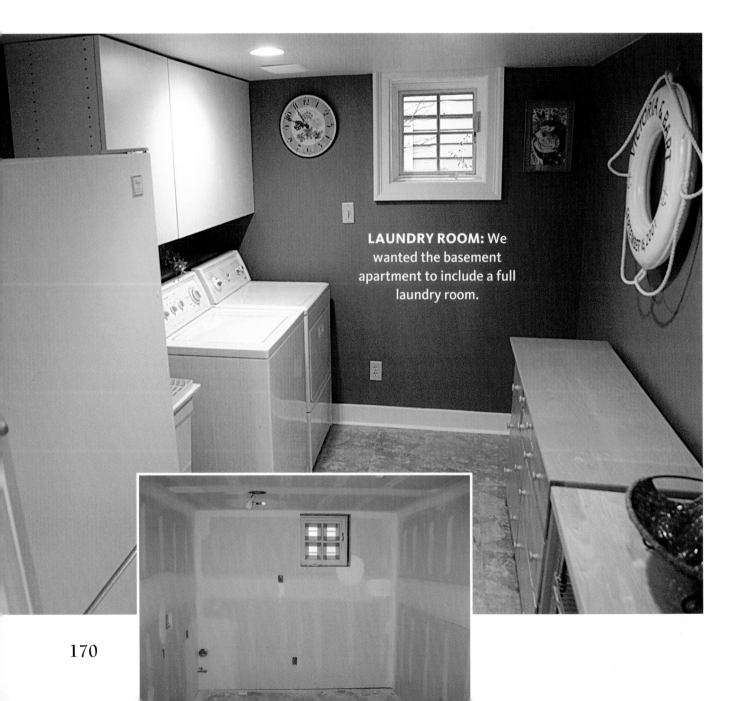

LAUNDRY ROOM: We wanted the basement apartment to include a full laundry room.

don't stick once the paint dries. The problem with a stuck window is that you may not realize it is painted shut until long after the job is finished. A professional painter will know how to avoid stuck windows. But if you are doing the job yourself, there are a number of sources, including information from paint manufacturers and suppliers, which show the right way to paint a window. The technique involves pulling the top sash down and the bottom one up to expose all of the paintable surfaces, then periodically moving the sash up and down until the paint dries completely.

Sticky windows can be fixed to open more smoothly by rubbing a bar of soap or a beeswax candle on the inside edges of the window where the paint wants to stick. There are also spray-on products for this purpose.

Factory-primed molding and window and door casings saved us time and labor on the job site.

Learning Curve

The Expensive View

It's interesting how you can fool yourself into thinking that you need something that you actually don't. This is especially true midconstruction when the full picture of how things will eventually look is not yet clear. This is how we ended up with three lovely (and pricy) skylights in the attic—not exactly the most accessible place for taking in the view. But when the rafters were rising, and the top of the house was open, the view from that part of the house was stunning. Why not add one more skylight? OK! Maybe we could change the plan a little, and create a different access so that we could put a chair up there?

Today, when I go into the laundry room, pull down the attic ladder, and climb up into that 8 x 4-foot space containing a furnace and three skylights, I'm reminded of the extra money we spent. But I'm not too hard on myself because almost every time I go up, I look out of one of those skylights, take a deep breath, and enjoy the scenery. "Hey, I think I can see Mount Rainier!"

Cabinetry and Countertops

Cabinetry is furniture that is truly a permanent fixture within your home. So before you lament about the cost of cabinetry—and you will—understand that it is a high-quality item. The average kitchen-cabinetry investment ranges from $8,000 to $15,000, and it is very easy to go higher than that. When you add in countertops, you will spend even more.

There are a number of options for remodelers when it comes to cabinetry. They include

1. **Resurfacing.** A veneer is added to existing cabinets to upgrade their appearance. Resurfacing your cabinets or replacing only the doors will typically save you about 25 percent of the cost of full replacement. However, you'll still have the same labor and installation expenses.

2. **Door Replacement.** In this case, the original cabinet "boxes" are retained, while new doors and hardware are added.

3. **Adding On.** New cabinets are purchased to match already existing cabinets. These new cabinets are intended to extend a row of existing cabinets and/or fill a new space with an exact replica of your already installed cabinets.

4. **Replacement.** All-new cabinets are installed.

We replaced our cabinets, and that is what is covered here. But if you are considering another option, remember that refacing and door replacement options assume that your cabinet boxes are still in good shape. If they aren't, or you want to take advantage of some of the extras that new cabinets offer, replace them. If you want to mix new cabinets with existing ones, make sure that the new units match the old in size and style.

Cabinet Sources. Where you purchase your new kitchen cabinets and who installs them can have a significant impact on your ability to successfully manage the process and achieve a satisfactory outcome. This is one area where the bidding process is particularly important. Don't rely solely on price. I used a local cabinet company

Order new kitchen cabinets when the framing is complete.

Unfinished cabinets, above and left, can be installed and then finished on-site. Remove the doors for any finishing work.

because they came to my house, took the necessary measurements, and provided drawings of the cabinet layout. They also took full responsibility that the new cabinets would fit within the kitchen per the remodel plan.

When you use the design assistance offered by a professional cabinet supplier, you rely on the company's expertise to help you navigate through a sea of difficult and challenging issues. With its knowledge, you can design an appropriate and affordable cabinetry solution that will take into account all of the variables, such as ceiling heights, appliance requirements, existing cabinetry if any, and the countertop you plan to use.

Today, it's rare to use a custom cabinetmaker to build the cabinet boxes unless you have an unusual circumstance. Most cabinet suppliers will customize a basic box to suit your needs.

Quality Check. Cabinet installation includes the setting and shimming of base cabinet boxes, and hanging wall cabinet boxes, both of which should be level and square. The addition of cabinet faces and all trim pieces such as crown molding, toe kicks, and fillers are installed. If necessary, the installer will make cutouts for appliances. Once the boxes are set, the countertop is added, and hinges, gliders, and finished doors and drawers are installed. Cabinet handles and knobs are installed last. Doors should open and close easily and sit squarely in the opening. Cabinets should be installed a minimum of 2 inches away from door frames to allow for countertop overhang.

Our kitchen cabinets include a few with glass doors for display and corner units where appropriate.

Other Types of Cabinetry. With a good finish carpenter on hand, the HGC can incorporate all sorts of custom and custom-look cabinetry into their project. For example, it's now popular to modify preexisting furniture, such as a buffet or side table, into a bathroom vanity or some other use. In many cases, the original top can be replaced with a more water resistant surface or sealed with polyurethane to protect the wood. To convert a piece of furniture to a vanity or kitchen sink, remove the drawers to make room for the sink and plumbing, but keep drawer and door fronts where possible.

It's also fairly inexpensive to create mantels, bookshelves, TV cabinets, or other fixtures out of pressboard, which when professionally painted looks like wood. Such fixtures can be added to existing areas or incorporated within stud bays during framing.

Countertops. There are as many countertop choices as there are cabinetry choices, which is why it's so important to understand your options and chose a design direction early in your construction planning. Even though the countertop is part of your cabinets, you will need a countertop fabricator to handle this part of the job. Your cabinet dealer can make recommendations.

COUNTERTOP MATERIALS

- Granite
- Marble
- Soapstone
- Engineered Stone
- Solid Surfacing
- Ceramic Tile
- Wood or Butcher Block
- Laminates
- Stainless Steel
- Concrete Counters

Granite tops the working surfaces in our kitchen, below left. Cabinets can include those for the kitchen as well as other spaces, below right.

Waterproof backer board, opposite, was applied under the tiles in our master bathroom shower.

Surfaces

Managing the installation of surfaces has more to do with picking the right materials and subcontractor than anything else. With tile installation, expect to have in-depth discussions with your tile setter while work is underway to clarify and evaluate design options for how the final pattern will look, and how edges, curves, or integration with other surfaces will be managed. As with other creative endeavors, what looks good on paper might not look great in reality. As the HGC you'll not only specify what type, size, quality, and quantity of material you want, but you'll also need to be on-site with your subcontractor to walk through the design layout. Do you want your tiles placed in a row, off-set, on-point (which means diagonally), or in another type of pattern, such as herringbone? Your tile setter can help you visualize how each of these layouts will look, but it's up to you to make the final decision and give the okay to complete the work. Discuss the base for each tile installation. Wet areas, such as tub walls, should be covered with cement backer board before tiling.

Wood Flooring. If you are integrating new wood flooring with pre-existing wood flooring, you'll need to discuss with your flooring installer how that transition should look. Other areas to discuss with this subcontractor are the thickness, type, and quality of materials, and the final finish of the floor—specifically, how many coats of finish will be applied and the type and quality of that finish. All of this should be spelled out in advance in your contract.

Crossing the Finish Line

Congratulations! Most of your work is done and you're now in the home stretch. This phase of construction is dedicated to finishing, finessing, and obtaining the final sign-offs on all of your remaining construction permits.

For the HGC, this is also the most pressure-filled time. Because the majority of payments have already been made, the motivation of your contractors to complete the work—or even show up—is at an all-time low. In fact, you might be experiencing a little burnout yourself. Moreover, be-

Staying on top of your subcontractors in this last phase is important. Their minds are already on their next project, and should you fail any final inspections, you might need them to return to complete additional work.

cause your remodeling budget at this late stage has been reduced to a trickle, you'll need to be especially careful about where and how you spend the remainder.

The 10/90 Rule. It's often said that the final 10 percent of construction work takes 90 percent of the time. This is not because the work is difficult, but because there are so many details that require attention. In the earlier stages of construction, such as excavation, framing, plumbing rough-in, and drywall, progress was obvious. You could actually see forward motion each day. Not so much anymore.

In the final phase, interior work involves finish carpentry, painting, and trim-out of plumbing, electrical, and mechanical systems. Your finish carpenter, who was on-site earlier, has now returned to finish up the trimwork and re-hang the doors so that they close and latch properly.

The Punch List. Because there are so many details, a good HGC writes up a comprehensive punch list that outlines all the remaining tasks required to finish the project. This punch list may contain all sorts of odds and ends—from replacing the screws on a drain grate to touching up paint, removing tape gum from window, or hanging curtain rods. Don't be surprised if a few small tasks are left for you to complete yourself.

If your family has lived elsewhere during construction, the good news is that it's time to come home. You might not have an entirely finished house, but if it's livable, it makes economic sense to move back in. The fact that your home is still something of a construction zone will motivate you to complete things more quickly.

Almost finished. At the very end of the project, your plumber will return to install all fixtures and fittings, such as bathroom and kitchen faucets.

Learning Curve

Tossing Out the To-Do List

The last-minute punch list thing did not go over well with my husband, Bart. It had been a long year of work, and now, with the finish line in sight, he had way more to do than he liked.

While my list included some paperwork and a few minor tasks, his involved caulking guns, hammers, fence repairs, and in almost every instance, hours of precious weekend time. Inevitably, he reached a tipping point. He flat-out refused to do one more thing, not even install a toilet paper holder.

After a few frustrating weeks of this impasse, we took the advice of a mutual friend and agreed to a three-month "time out" from working on the house. That was good advice. Now, two years later, we can laugh at that punch list. We managed to check items off over time, keep our marriage intact, and still finish everything on the list—well, almost everything.

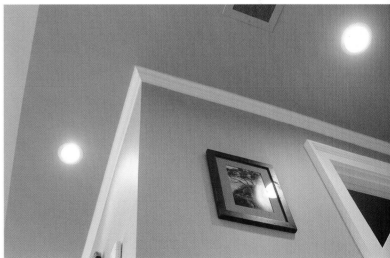

Hardwood flooring, left, can be installed before the painting phase. Plan on controlling dust raised by floor sanding.

Lighting fixtures, above, such as lenses, sconces, and chandeliers, are among the last items to be installed.

What May be Left

Odds and Ends. All interior trim is added, caulked, and painted. Built-ins are completed. Finished interior doors and cabinets are installed, as is hardware such as handles and knobs. Countertops are completed and installed. All stair railings, banisters, and decks are installed and finished in place.

Plumbing, Fixtures, and Electrical Trim-Out. Sinks, toilets, faucets, and showerheads are installed, and water pressure is tested. Towel racks, toilet paper holders, and mirrors are mounted. Outlets are wired, switch covers added, electrical fans, doorbells, security systems, speakers, and smoke detectors are mounted and connected. The circuit breaker box is labeled.

Quality Check. After all the fixtures are installed, make sure your plumber tests the water pressure right away to see if any leaks show up. Where high water pressure is a concern, your plumber should install a regulator after the test is complete. Inspectors check and approve final work on your plumbing, electrical, and mechanical systems and signs off on the trade permits.

Outside. Once the majority of interior construction is complete, you'll start working on the outside of your home. Shutters and window boxes are hung. House numbers, outside lights, and outlets are mounted; masonry restoration, garage doors, and door openers are installed; and paint and caulking touchups are completed.

You'll manage basic cleanup and then discontinue the use of dumpsters. Portable toilet facilities should now be removed along with any temporary fences that have been installed to keep the property protected during construction.

Money-Saving Tip. The excavation work performed during your project should have prepared your yard not only for new walkways and driveways, but also for the ultimate configuration of your yard and gardens. The latter is particularly important. Even if you do not have the resources to install landscaping immediately after your remodel, completing the excavation as part of your flatwork project will save you from paying for it later.

Take the time to remove the scars of construction from your property for the sake of your long-suffering neighbors, who've most likely had to endure the loss of parking spots, the noise of hammering, sawing, and swearing, and all sorts of fallout from your ambitious project. Landscaping does not have to be ostentatious or expensive. A simple lawn with a small, well-tended garden can make the difference between a professional job and an uninspired conclusion.

Today, when I look at my remodeled home, I puff up a little—as you will, too, once your own work is complete. Interestingly, it's when I approach my house—from the back alley after taking the trash out, or up the walkway from a stroll around the neighborhood—that I most admire it. There it sits, guarded by a pair of golden chain trees and fringed by bergenias, camellias, and a star magnolia. Its brass house numbers, new green paint job, and brave turret all seem to say, "Good job. Well done." And best of all, "Welcome home." ❧

Finish up, opposite and below, by attending to the details that make your project stand out, such as planting window boxes and your garden.

APPENDIX: SAMPLE CONTRACT

FRAMING SUBCONTRACTOR AGREEMENT

Owner   **Project Address**   **Architect**
  Bart and Victoria Likes   Anywhere, USA   Pete Sandall

Contractor
  Company Name   ACME Framing Construction
  Owner Name   Mr. Framer
  Address
  Phone
  Fax
  Liability Insurance Carrier   Umi Insurance Company
  Contractor License #

Bid and Payment
  Amount of Bid: $37,200
  Work Start Date: Estimated: [date]
  Work Completion Date: Estimated: [date]
  Payment Terms: $3,720 to commence work and 4 subsequent payments—based on per centage of work complete, to be invoiced and paid as work progresses. Final payment due upon completion and final sign off of finish.

JOB SPECIFICATIONS

All framing work to be completed per the approved building and framing plans—including shear wall schedule, hold-down schedule, and floor and roof framing plan notes. Subcontractor will use provided materials, as specified in the supplied blueprints. Approximately 20 hours of miscellaneous demolition is included in the cost of this bid. Unused demo hours to be credited back to owner.

LOWER FLOOR PLAN
• Frame all interior walls.
• Frame new exterior walls @ addition.
• Frame new walls to fur out old foundation walls.
• Install Firestop between new furred out exterior walls and existing exterior walls.
• Frame in old stair opening.
• Cut in new stair opening in existing joist.
• Install new hardware @ floor joist to bring up to new shear wall schedule.
• Frame in new stairs (REVISED).
• Frame gas fireplace box, as specified in product installation materials (NEW).
• Cut window openings as needed/install windows per manufacturer specification for all new lower-floor windows (NEW).

MAIN FLOOR
• Frame new floor @ addition.

• Frame new addition walls.
• Frame new walls @ pantry, kitchen, bath, pass-through room, closet, and stairs (REVISED).
• Frame new short wall (w/expanded arch) between existing living room/old dining room. (NEW).
• Cut new stir opening in existing floor joist.
• Frame new stairs.
• Frame up new columns and door surround outside of front door (REVISED).
• Frame gas fireplace box, as specified in product installation materials (NEW).
• Frame raised hearth for gas fireplace in great room (NEW).
• Install new exterior sheathing @ existing exterior walls to bring up to new shear wall schedule.
• Install new hardware @ floor joist to bring up to new shear wall schedule.
• Cut window openings as needed/install windows per manufacturer specification for all main floor windows (NEW).
• Re-install existing front door (NEW).
• Install new exterior French doors in new dining room (west exposure) (NEW).

MAIN FLOOR DECK
The following work to be accomplished per owner-provided plan and instruction. This will be a tiled deck w/ slope and drainage system. Concrete piers and brackets, iron balusters, and top rails to be installed by others.

- Install deck flashing and sloped deck joist (ledger to be approximately 2" below interior floor height) on the west exterior of the house per owner-provided plan and specified height. Installation to include galvanized washers between ledger and house for drainage (NEW).
- Install 8" x 8" pressure-treated posts on pre-poured concrete piers for new deck (NEW).
- Install 8" x 8" pressure-treated beams w/ 2x12 joists—16" on center (NEW).
- Install sloped deck surface (pressure-treated plywood), using ½" bolts every 10" (NEW).
- Install sloped pressure-treated stairs, and landings per plan, to ground level (NEW).

UPPER FLOOR
- Frame new floor.
- Frame new exterior and interior walls.
- Frame ceiling detail at master bedroom.
- Frame wall arch over main bathtub area (NEW).
- Frame gas fireplace box, as specified in product installation materials (NEW).
- Install exterior flashing and door in master bedroom—threshold flashing, and deck flashing to be provided and installed by others (NEW).
- Install windows per manufacturer specification for all upper floor windows (NEW).

UPPER FLOOR DECK
- Install sloped blocked floor joists for upper deck (REVISED)
- Install ¾" plywood supply ACX over sloped blocked floor joists (NEW).

ATTIC
- Install attic floor (NEW).

ROOF
- Install trusses and sheet with plywood.
- Install rafters @ front of house and sheet with plywood as specified per plan (REVISED).
- Frame enclosed soffit (no trim).
- Install fascia and barge trim only.
- Cut out roof openings and install skylight in master bath, as indicated per plan (NEW).
- Cut out roof openings and install tube skylights in laundry room, closet and main bath, as indicated per plan (NEW).
- Cut all roof vents.

GARAGE
- Frame new exterior walls and sheet with plywood (REVISED).
- Install trusses and sheet with plywood.
- Frame enclosed soffit.
- Install windows on north exposure, as specified per plan.
- Cut all roof vents.

SUBCONTRACTOR-SPECIFIED PROVISIONS OF AGREEMENT
1. Rough frame house and garage @ XXX Ave Seattle, WA.
2. Price includes installation of all framing hardware, hold downs, straps, hangers, etc. as specified in the permitted plans for this project.
3. Price includes flashing installation and wrapping window openings with moist stop paper (REVISED).
4. Price includes the installation of all windows and exterior doors (REVISED).
5. Owner to provide all lumber, framing hardware, window wrap, flashing, and any other building materials needed to complete this job.
6. Nails are additional and will be billed as used.
7. Crane time is additional, and will be billed if used. (Requires owner agreement prior to ordering crane.)
8. Does not include any setting of interior doors.
9. Cost is subject to accuracy of architects plans.
10. Non-refundable down payment if work is cancelled.
11. Payments are due on or before the 10th of the month for work done in the previous month until finished.
12. Owner accepts the ACME Framing Construction Contract Terms and Conditions, provided on 7/8/05.
13. Agreed Upon Square Footage:
    i.   Main and Upper Floor: 2,219
    ii. Basement: 1,200
    iii. Garage: 330

OWNER-SPECIFIED PROVISIONS OF AGREEMENT
1. All work will meet quality workmanship standards and building code requirements.
2. All materials will be new, unless otherwise agreed to in writing.
3. All materials and labor shall be warranted for a minimum of one year.
4. Contractor will install all products per manufacturer installation procedures and recommendations. Contractor accepts liability for any void of product warranty for improper installation.
5. Contractor agrees to maintain all applicable insurance policies for the duration of this project. In the event existing insurance policies expire during the construction period, contractor will provide renewal certificates as of the day of the previous policy cancellation before further payments will be made.
6. Contractor will add owner as additional insured on contractor's liability insurance policy for this project.

Agreed to by the following on : _____
                                        (Date)

_____   _____
Victoria Likes/Owner   Contractor – Mr. Framer

NOTE: This is an abbreviated list of provisions. The original contract contained 25 provisions. For a list of provisions to include in your contracts, see "Creating a Binding Contract," page 72.

RESOURCE GUIDE

This list of manufacturers and associations is meant to be a general guide to additional industry and product-related sources. It is not intended as a listing of products and manufacturers represented by the photographs in this book.

ASSOCIATIONS

American Architectural Manufacturers Association
1540 E. Dundee Rd., Ste. 310
Palatine, IL 60067
708-202-1350
www.aamanet.org
Organization of window, door, and skylight manufacturers.

American Gas Association
400 N. Capitol St., NW
Washington, DC 20001
202-824-7000
www.aga.org
Clearinghouse for gas energy information, including data on appliances and energy efficiency.

APA – The Engineered Wood Association
7011 South 19th
Tacoma, WA 98466
253-565-6600
www.apawood.org
Nonprofit trade association that provides information on engineered wood products.

AWCI – The Association of the Wall and Ceiling Industries International
803 West Broad St., Ste. 600
Falls Church, VA 22046
703-534-8300
www.awci.org
Provides services and information for building contractors.

Carpet and Rug Institute
P.O. Box 2048, 310 Holiday Ave.
Dalton, GA 30720-2048
800-882-8846
www.carpet-rug.com
Provides guidelines for consumers on carpet/rug selection, installation, daily maintenance, and long-term care.

Center for Universal Design
N.C. State University
College of Design
Campus Box 7701
Raleigh, NC 27695-7701
www.design.ncsu.edu
The Center for Universal Design promotes design that accommodates people with ranges of physical ability.

Ceramic Tile Institute of America, Inc.
12061 W. Jefferson Blvd.
Culver City, CA 90230-6219
310-574-7800
www.ctioa.org
Membership trade organization promoting the tile industry.

Home Ventilating Institute
30 W. University Dr.
Arlington Heights, IL 60004
847-394-0150
www.hvi.org
Non-profit association that provides consumer information on home ventilating products.

National Electrical Manufacturers Association

1300 N. 17th St., Ste. 1847
Rosslyn, VA 22209
703-841-3200
www.nema.org
Helps consumers select safe, reliable electrical equipment.

National Fire Protection Association

1 Batterymarch Pk.
Quincy, MA 02169-7471
800-344-3555
www.nfpa.org
Nonprofit organization providing fire safety information to the public.

International Code Council

5203 Leesburg Pike, Ste. 600
Falls Church, VA 22041
703-931-4533
www.iccsafe.org
Provides construction codes and standards used on job sites.

NAHB – National Association of Home Builders

1201 15th St., NW
Washington, DC 20005
800-368-5242
www.nahb.org
Trade association that promotes and provides information on the home-building industry.

North American Insulation Manufacturers Association (NAIMA)

44 Canal Center Plaza, Ste. 310
Alexandria, VA 22314
703- 684-0084
www.naima.org
North American trade association of manufacturers of fiberglass, rock wool, and slag wool insulation products.

National Association of the Remodeling Industry (NARI)

780 Lee St., Ste. 200
Des Plaines, IL 60016
800-611-6274
www.nari.org
Professional organization providing information for contractors, remodelers, and designers.

National Kitchen and Bath Association (NKBA)

687 Willow Grove St.
Hackettstown, NJ 07840
800-843-6522
www.nkba.org
National trade organization that provides remodeling information and a designer referral service for consumers.

Plumbing Manufacturers Institute

1340 Remington Rd., Ste. A
Schaumburg, IL 60173
847-884-9764
www.pmihome.org
Not-for-profit national trade association of manufacturers of plumbing products.

Southern Forest Products Association

P.O. Box 641700
Kenner, LA 70064
504-443-4464
www.sfpa.org
Marketing organization for Southern Pine forest products.

Timber Framers Guild

P.O. Box 60
Becket, MA 01223
888-453-0879
www.tfguild.org
Organization dedicated to providing training and information for timber framers.

Window & Door Manufacturer's Association

1400 E. Touhy Ave., Ste. 470
Des Plaines, IL 60018
800-223-2301
www.wdma.com
Promotes high-performance standards for windows, skylights, and doors.

Tile Council of America, Inc.

100 Clemson Research Blvd.
Anderson, SC 29625
864-646-8453
www.tileusa.com
Association offering consumers information on selecting and installing tile.

MANUFACTURERS

American Standard

1 Centennial Plaza, P. O. Box 6820
Piscataway, NJ 08855-6820
www.americanstandard-us.com
Manufactures plumbing and tile products.

Armstrong World Industries

2500 Columbia Ave.
P.O. Box 3001
Lancaster, PA 17604
800-233-3823
www.armstrong.com
Manufactures floors, cabinets, and ceilings for both home and commercial use.

Andersen Corporation

100 Fourth Ave.
North Bayport, MN 55003-1096
800-426-4261
www.andersoncorp.com
Manufacturer of windows.

Bosch Home Appliances

5551 McFadden Ave.
Huntington Beach, CA 92807
714-901-6600
www.boschappliances.com
Manufactures major and small appliances.

CaesarStone USA

6840 Hayvenhurst Ave., Ste. 100
Van Nuys, CA 91406
818-779-0999
www.caesarstoneus.com
Manufactures quartz-composite countertops.

Corian, a div. of DuPont

Chestnut Run Plaza
721 Maple Run
P.O. Box 80721

Wilmington, DE 19880

800-426-7426

www.corian.com

Manufactures solid-surfacing material for home and commercial kitchens.

Delta Faucet Co.

55 E. 111th St.

P.O. Box 40980

Indianapolis, IN 46280

317-848-1812

www.deltafaucet.com

Manufactures a variety of faucets and finishes for kitchen and bath.

Elkay

2222 Camden Ct.

Oak Brook, IL 60523

630-574-8484

www.elkayusa.com

Manufactures sinks, faucets, and countertops.

Fisher and Paykel

5900 Skylab Rd.

Huntington Beach, CA 92647

888-936-7872

www.fisherandpaykel.com

Manufactures kitchen appliances.

Forbo Flooring US

866-Marmoleum

www.forbo.com

Manufactures Marmoleum brand flooring.

Formica Corporation

225 E. 5th St., Ste. 200

Cincinnati, OH 45202

800-367-6422

www.formica.com

Manufacturer of laminate and solid-surfacing material.

Frigidaire

P.O. Box 212378

Martinez, GA 30917

800-374-4432

www.frigidaire.com

Manufacturers major appliances, including ranges, cook-tops, refrigerators, and dishwashers.

General Electric

800-626-2000

www.geappliances.com

Manufactures refrigerators, dishwashers, ovens, and other major appliances.

GAF Materials Corporation

1361 Alps Rd.

Wayne, NJ 07470

800-ROOF-411

www.gaf.com

Manufacturer of commercial and residential roofing materials.

Murphy Bed Company

42 Central Ave.

Farmingdale, NY 11735

800-845-2337

www.murphybedcompany.com

Manufactures Murphy beds, which save space by tipping up into a self-contained wall unit.

National Manufacturing Company

P.O. Box 577

Sterling, IL 61081-0577

800-346-9445

www.natman.com

Leading supplier of home, farm, and builder's hardware products to the retail home-improvement industry.

GLOSSARY

Actual dimension (lumber) The exact cross-sectional measurements of a piece of lumber after it has been cut, surfaced, and dried.

Asphalt shingle Shingles made of felt that has been soaked in asphalt; asphalt shingle tabs are coated with granular minerals.

Backfill Soil or gravel used to fill in between a finished foundation and the ground excavated around it.

Blocking 1) Horizontal blocks inserted between studs every 10 vertical feet to defeat the spread of fire. 2) Lumber added between studs, joists, rafters, or other members to provide a nailing surface for sheathing or other material.

Board foot Unit of volume for a piece of wood 12 inches square and 1 inch thick.

Bridging Wood blocks installed in an X-shape between floor joists to stabilize and position the joists.

Caulk Tube-delivered plastic-and-silicon substance that cures quickly and is used to seal gaps in wood to prevent air or water leakage.

Check (in lumber) A defect in lumber caused by a separation lengthwise between the wood's growth rings.

Chords In triangular trusses, the wood members that form the two sides of the roof and the triangle's base.

Cleat A small board fastened to a surface to provide support for another board.

Cricket A small gable-like structure installed on a roof to divert water, usually from a chimney.

Crosscuts Cuts made width-wise, or across the grain of lumber.

Crown The natural bow along the edge of a joist, rafter, stair stringer, or other member.

Dormer A shed- or doghouse-like structure that projects from a roof and can add space to an attic.

Double top plate The double tier of two-by lumber running horizontally on top of and nailed to wall studs.

Drywall Gypsum sandwiched between treated paper. Used as an interior covering material.

Elevation The same as height. When referred to in transit use, the height above or below a transit instrument.

Fire blocking Horizontal blocking installed between studs to defeat the upward progress of fire.

Floor plans Drawings that give a plan view (bird's-eye view) of the layout of each floor of a building.

Footing The base, usually poured concrete, on which a foundation wall is built. With a pressure-treated wood foundation, a gravel or soil footing may be used.

Framing anchor Metal straps, pockets, or supports used to reinforce or strengthen joints between wood framing members.

Ground-fault circuit interrupter (GFCI) A device that detects a ground fault or electrical line leakage and immediately shuts down power.

I-beam A beam, typically steel, with a vertical middle section and flat webs on the top and bottom.

Joist Framing lumber placed on edge horizontally, to which subfloors or ceilings are attached.

Oriented-strand board (OSB) Panel material made of wood strands purposely aligned for strength and bonded by phenolic resin.

Platform framing The framing method that builds walls, one story at a time, on top of platforms that are built on joists.

Plumb Vertically straight. A line 90 degrees to a level line.

Prehung door A door that's already set in a jamb, with hinges (and sometimes a lockset) preinstalled, ready to be installed in a rough opening.

Pressure treatment A factory process of using pressure to force preservatives into wood.

Pump jack A working platform system that is raised and lowered along vertical 4x4s using a pumping action.

Shear wall A wall, typically covered with carefully nailed plywood, which is designed to resist lateral force.

Sheathing Panel material, typically plywood, applied to the outside of a structure on which siding is installed.

Soffit The board that runs the length of a wall, spanning between the wall and the fascia on the underside of the rafters.

Stud Vertically standing two-by lumber that extends from the bottom plate to the top plate of a stud wall.

Subfloor Structurally rated plywood or oriented-strand-board decking installed on sleepers or joists.

Trim One-by lumber used as siding corner boards or as finish materials around windows and doors, under eaves, or around cornices.

Warp Uneven shrinkage in wood causing bending or twisting.

Web (truss) The truss's inner members that tie together the chords.

INDEX

Have a home improvement, decorating, or gardening project? Look for these and other fine Creative Homeowner books wherever books are sold.

The complete manual for plumbing projects. Over 750 color photos and illustrations. 288 pp.; $8^{1}/_{2}$" × $10^{7}/_{8}$"
BOOK #: 278200

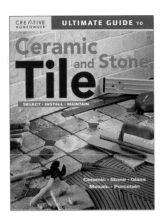

Complete DIY tile instruction. Over 550 color photos and illustrations. 224 pp.; $8^{1}/_{2}$" × $10^{7}/_{8}$"
BOOK #: 277532

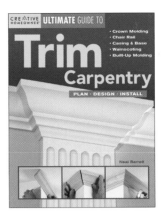

Add trimwork and molding to your home. Over 700 photos and illustrations. 208 pp.; $8^{1}/_{2}$" × $10^{7}/_{8}$"
BOOK #: 277516

The ultimate home-improvement reference manual. Over 300 step-by-step projects. 608 pp.; 9" × $10^{7}/_{8}$"
BOOK #: 267870

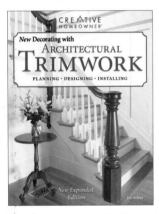

Transform a room with trimwork. Over 550 color photos and illustrations. 240 pp.; $8^{1}/_{2}$" × $10^{7}/_{8}$"
BOOK #: 277500

Complete source book for molding trim. 1,000+ color photos and illos. 256 pp.; $8^{1}/_{2}$" × $10^{7}/_{8}$"
BOOK #: 279402

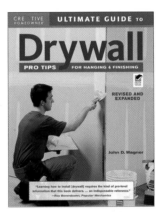

A complete guide, covering all aspects of drywall. Over 450 color photos. 160 pp.; $8^{1}/_{2}$" × $10^{7}/_{8}$"
BOOK #: 278320

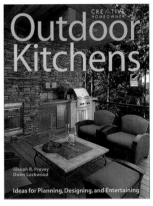

Planning and design advice from top professionals. Over 335 photos. 224 pp.; $8^{1}/_{2}$" × $10^{7}/_{8}$"
BOOK #: 277571

New edition, with all the answers for a new kitchen. Over 500 color photographs. 224 pp.; $8^{1}/_{2}$" × $10^{7}/_{8}$"
BOOK #: 279412

Interior design with eco-friendly materials. Over 200 color photos. 208 pp.; $8^{1}/_{2}$" × $10^{7}/_{8}$"
BOOK #: 279062

An impressive guide to garden design and plant selection. 950 color photos and illustrations. 384 pp.; 9" × 10"
BOOK #: 274610

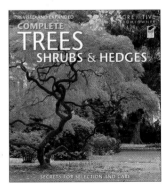

How to select and care for landscaping plants. More than 700 photos. 240 pp.; 9" × 10"
BOOK #: 274222

For more information and to order direct, visit our Web site at **www.creativehomeowner.com**